FRONTIERS IN MUSLIM-CHRISTIAN ENCOUNTER

FRONTIERS IN MUSLIM-CHRISTIAN ENCOUNTER

Michael Nazir-Ali

OXFORD
REGNUM BOOKS

The publishers express their thanks to Jeremy Mudditt of Paternoster Press for his advice and to John Waters for his editorial assistance.

Regnum Books is a two-thirds world publishing company publishing on behalf of the African Theological Fraternity, the Latin American Theological Fraternity, and Partnership in Mission Asia. It works in co-operation with major western Christian organisations and is based at the Oxford Centre for Mission Studies, P.O. Box 70, Oxford, U.K.

British Library Cataloguing in Publication Data

Nazir-Ali, Michael
Frontiers in Muslim Christian encounter.
1. Christianity and other religions—Islam
2. Islam—Relations—Christianity
I. Title
200 BP172

ISBN 1–870345–05–3

Typeset by Photoprint, 9–11 Alexandra Lane, Torquay, Devon, and printed by A. Wheaton & Co. Ltd., Exeter, for Regnum Books, P.O. Box 70, Oxford, U.K.

Contents

Foreword

I first met Bishop Michael Nazir-Ali more than 20 years ago in Pākistān, and began a friendship that has transcended many experiences and separations since. Islām has always been the social and cultural context of our meeting and has influenced the way in which our partnership in the Gospel has been shared. Michael's own family roots are found in Islām, offering him a very special preparation for a lifetime of sensitive and informed comment and dialogue. In an earlier book *Islām—A Christian Perspective* he explores the early formation of Islām, its rapid cultural, social and theological development and identifies its modern trends and dilemmas. In such a framework he opens up the question of the 'Christian presence' and begins the exploration that leads to this new book. In *Frontiers in Muslim-Christian Encounter* there is a natural extension into theology, missiology and dialogue that meets a significant need in the literature and demonstrates vividly the potential in risking an encounter on such a crucial frontier.

Many years ago Kenneth Cragg, in his classic *Call of the Minaret*, made a plea for a serious attempt to 're-interpret' the Gospel in terms that could be understood by Muslims. He wrote:

> 'If Christ is what Christ is, he must be uttered. If Islām is what Islām is, that "must" is irresistible. Wherever there is misconception, witness must penetrate, wherever there is obscuring of the beauty of the Cross, it must be unveiled; wherever men have missed God in Christ, he must be brought to them again . . . We must present Christ, for the sole sufficient reason that he deserves to be presented.'

It is the quality of our loving kindness and the patient witness of our lives that will open the way and the mind to enable the message of Jesus to be received. Despite more than a decade in Asia and the Middle East I have yet to meet a Muslim who has been convinced and persuaded by the quality of our arguments or by the extent of our knowledge to follow the Jesus of the Gospels. Rather that transformation has only ever been born out of the miracle of love translated into theology, life and witness by the power of the Holy Spirit in our lives. I do not mean to be presumptuous in saying that this book seeks to demonstrate this understanding and succeeds admirably.

This is especially clear in the way that *Muḥammad Iqbāl*'s thought and philosophy is presented in the final section of Chapter 1. *Iqbāl*, the post-philosopher of the nation of Pākistān, has seldom been given the place he deserves by writers on the sub-continent but is of considerable significance when Christology is examined within the Islāmic context, and as a bridge to understanding and communication. The cult of Prophet veneration in a later section also offers an unusual insight into the real Islām of the villages, and at the same time provides a way into the hearts and aspirations of those who seek a Saviour and have yet to find one.

In *Frontiers in Muslim-Christian Encounter* the reader is drawn into the meaning of Christ for those living within a Muslim environment. It is an important encounter, but with Christ as he is, and Islām so demanding, it will bring an incalculable reward.

ARCHBISHOP DAVID PENMAN,
Melbourne, Australia.

Introduction
Christian Worship, Witness and Work in Islāmic Contexts; Directions in Mission*

Christian presence in the Islāmic world is as varied in character as it is changing. It ranges from substantial minorities in some countries to hardly any Christians at all in others. In many countries the Christian presence is ancient, considerably older than the presence of Islām. In others it is comparatively recent, dating from the first arrival of European traders or colonists in that part of the world.

In some parts of the Islāmic world, particularly the Middle East, the Christian presence is experiencing a decline in numbers—mainly through emigration to North America, Europe and Australia. Such a decline could, in the long run, affect the nature of Christian witness in this part of the world. Elsewhere, Christians are growing numerically and this growth in numbers is changing their role in wider society. There are parts of the Islāmic world where Christians are relatively free to worship and to witness, but there are also countries where such worship and witness are severely restricted. In some countries, the Christian presence is indigenous, while in others it may be mainly expatriate.

These conditions influence the ways in which Christians worship and witness in their particular context in the Islāmic world. For

*Published in the special 75th anniversary issue of the *International Review of Mission*.

example, the ancient Churches, because of the restrictions on them in the past, have developed a theology of witness which emphasizes the centrality of the eucharistic liturgy in Christian witness. This is not surprising since the liturgy was often the only way in which they could declare their faith. There were periods of greater freedom when scholars could debate with each other on religious matters and forthright religious discussion was even possible in the court. Liturgy, nevertheless, remained not only the central act of worship but of witness as well. The movement for liturgical renewal has enabled the Church world-wide to gain this insight of the ancient Churches that liturgy can be an act of witness and even of proclamation. On the part of the ancient Churches, a rediscovery of the Bible, along with changed circumstances, has led to the revival of preaching in some of these Churches in Islāmic countries. This mutual renewal is one of the most valuable aspects of the ecumenical movement.

While reaffirming the necessity of proclaiming Jesus Christ as Lord and Saviour of all humankind, the context in which we carry out an evangelization must be considered. A great deal has been written about the inculturation or contextualization of the Gospel in Muslim countries. This valuable work needs to be affirimed as it weighs the 'translatibility'[1] of the Christian faith against the resistance of Islām to such a process. Islām, despite its firm roots in one cultural tradition, aspires to be international in character (hence the current popularity of the pan-Islāmic movements). Christians in a Muslim context should go beyond the indigenization or contextualization of mission to the 'internationalization' of it. In other words the 'loss of nerve' in Christian mission which has accompanied the decline of Western imperialism should be countered not by merely encouraging 'national' Churches to engage in mission (though this is important), but by freeing Christian mission from the hegemony of the West so that mission can once again be 'from everywhere to everywhere'. For example, it would be valuable for cross-cultural workers to go from one Islāmic context to another. An Arab evangelist can make a significant impact in Pākistān; Indonesian missionaries in Bangladesh would be a tremendous tonic for the small Church there. Western Churches, voluntary societies and ecumenical bodies can become effective facilitators in this process instead of just carrying on with a token gesture here and there.[2]

The resources which go into training, sending and maintaining Western missionaries are enormous. Sensitive Christians, aware of the tremendous material and spiritual needs of the world, are concerned about the spending of such large amounts on Christian workers. The sphere and term of service of such Christians abroad is increasingly circumscribed and their very presence may be counterproductive to the cause of Christian mission in some contexts. A moratorium would have the undesirable effect of creating 'national' Churches with only marginal awareness of the catholicity of the Church of Jesus Christ. One of the ways around this dilemma is to encourage cross-cultural mission from 'everywhere to everywhere'.

Another aspect of the 'internationalization' of Christian mission is study and research by regional and worldwide ecumenical organizations on Christian presence in Muslim contexts and carefully thought out articulation of the problems and opportunities this presents. Christians in Muslim contexts welcome the concern which ecumenical organizations have for justice and peace in many parts of the world. They recognize this as part of the biblical mandate for the Church, but such organizations fail to take commensurate interest in the Muslim world concerning matters of justice and peace.

The challenge of Liberation Theology is causing a shift in theological method: theology is increasingly being done 'from below'.[3] This means that both the biblical context and the contemporary context are being taken seriously in theological reflection. Contemporary conditions often highlight theological themes and their context in the Bible. This shift in theological method has profound implications for dialogue between Christians and those of other faiths. Theology can no longer be understood merely as the systematic elaboration of abstract doctrine, equally, inter-faith dialogue can no longer be understood merely as discussion about doctrines of the various faiths. Dialogue too must begin 'from below', with the actual situation affecting both the Christian and the interlocutor.

In Islāmic contexts, dialogue should address issues such as the importance given to human dignity and human rights by our respective traditions. What do they have to say about racial or sexual discrimination? How are the prophetic concerns for justice and mercy to be addressed to our own situation? In what ways do our traditions encourage reconciliation between communities? What respect is there for freedom of conscience, of belief and the freedom to alter one's belief? Are these who call themselves Muslims or Christians faithful to the witness of their tradition?

The existence of poverty in our world raises other issues: the problem of development, of an equitable economic order and the tyranny that rich nations exercise over poor ones. The existence of oppressive social systems and the peculiar mentality which they create among the oppressed highlights a further area for action. Profound theological issues regarding human nature, sinfulness, God's revelation of himself and of his will for humanity, divine involvement in human affairs, etc., will be brought into focus by a dialogue which begins from below. Theological belief or doctrine will thus have a logical but not necessarily a temporal priority for those who engage in dialogue. Temporal priority is to be given to the questions people ask which arise directly from their situations about life, relationships, the environment, and so on. Even in dialogue, however, doctrine does have logical priority, for each of us approaches a particular situation with our own assumptions and beliefs. Systematic theological reflection on dialogue may treat the theological issues arising from dialogue as prior for the sake of clarity and direction.

Inter-faith and cross-cultural encounters necessarily raise the question of contextualization or inculturation: how is Christian faith to be expressed so that those from another tradition may grasp its meaning and invitation? But such contextualization is not a mere disguise which leaves the Christian's values and understanding unaffected. The clothing of the Gospel in another cultural or religious tradition will also to some extent evangelize the evangelist as he discovers what aspects of the gospel are highlighted by the particular situation in which inculturation is taking place. Quoting from I Cor. 9:19–23, Kenneth Cracknell has this to say about such inculturation:

> 'In this way Paul speaks of what we today would call empathy and identification and of a deep loving concern for the other. In the last words (of the passage) we have what has been called 'the purest missionary motive of all'—we share in dialogue because we want to share in the blessings of the Gospel.'[4]

Such identification must have limits, however, if we are to be faithful followers of Christ. The history of the Church's efforts at inculturation is littered with attempts to discard such boundaries in the process of inculturation. Valid and even necessary limits to inculturation would certainly include faithfulness to Scripture and to Apostolic tradition. Scripture is the norm which has been given by God and adopted by the Church; it defines and preserves the people of God. Apostolic tradition ensures the continuity of a local church with the Church through the ages, and its contiguity with the contemporary Church world-wide. This does not mean that any one cultural understanding of Scripture or of tradition is to be accepted uncritically. Part of the work of contextualization is precisely to allow the context or contexts of Scripture to interact creatively with our contemporary contexts. The same may be said of Apostolic tradition. Creative and maybe radical reinterpretation of Scripture and tradition will surely result from such interaction. Scripture and tradition are normative precisely because they can interact in these creative ways with all given contexts.

Contextualization in Islāmic countries has certain special features which are worthy of note. In the first place, it must be recognized that Islām has had a dynamic and dialogical (in its widest sense) relationship with Christianity from its earliest days. This means that there are many cultural forms, systems of thought and beliefs which have a shared basis. This creates both opportunities and problems in that the terminology, life-style and architecture of the one can never be wholly strange to the other. From the Christian side in particular, the 'translation' of Christian faith into an Islāmic culture can be carried out in the knowledge that the forms being adopted and the terminology being used have, after all, some previous or current point of contact with Christianity. Problems arise when one side attempts to make exclusive to itself certain terminology or cultural forms, which, properly speaking, should be shared. A recent example of this is the ban which has been imposed in a South-east Asian country, on use by Christians of certain 'Islāmic' terms such as *Allāh* or *Ṣalāt* (ritual mandatory prayer). The term *Allāh* in particular has had a long and varied history and was extensively used in pre-Islāmic Arabia by all kinds of people. Arabic-speaking Christians to this day use it as their ordinary term for God; the Arabic Bible uses it regularly and consistently. The authorities of the country in question seem to identify Christianity with Western, and more particularly, Anglo-Saxon, culture. This may be understandable in the light of their recent colonial experience, but in terms of Islāmic history (where Christians are found to be ubiquitous), it is hardly convincing. A renewed emphasis on the indigeneity of Christian faith within Islāmic civilization as a whole must form part of the agenda for Muslim-Christian encounter in the coming years. In this area, the witness of our Oriental Orthodox and Catholic brethren is vitally important.[5]

Radical discipleship and humble service are another aspect of Christian witness which must be maintained and increased. From the earliest days of Islām, Christians have been known to play their part in the fields of education and medicine.[6] The modern missionary movement provided added impetus to this service. Today, Christians are involved in newer kinds of service, ranging from conscientization to sanitation.[1] The basis of all dialogue is loving, serving witness to our fellow man. The eucharistic liturgy is a celebration of the supreme service of self-giving. In the liturgy, our Lord gives himself to us so that we may give to others. Christians should always be on the alert for new ways to serve their fellow human beings. All such service should lead towards that restoration of wholeness and well being which is our Lord's will for all humanity; wholeness not only of individual men and women, but the restored wholeness of a human society fragmented by human greed, selfishness and obstinacy. Of course, the Church herself cannot bring about that complete transformation which is the Kingdom of God. That is God's work, but the Church can be a sign and a foretaste of it.

A rapidly changing world will always challenge Christians to consider and adopt new and more profound ways of serving society. Christians must not shirk this challenge. The Islāmic context may truly be described as one of 'poverty with pockets of affluence'.[7] Christian service in such a context will be as varied as the context itself. There will be continuing need for relief and development work in many Muslim lands; there will be need for witnessing for justice and equity. There will be need for conscientization; for making men and women aware of their dignity and their rights, for reconciliation and peace between communities. The role of the Christian Church in bringing about transformation in these areas can be crucial and significant.

Let us pray that the Church in the coming years will continue to proclaim and to celebrate the mystery of Christ; to incarnate herself in the varied contexts wherein she finds herself; to see, understand and persuade; to serve in humble invitation of her Lord. May all this be for the sake of and as a sign of the coming reign of God!

I dedicate this work to the memory of my late father, *James Nazir-Ali,* who has made this encounter possible.

Part I
Theology in Encounter

CHAPTER 1

The Christian Doctrine of God in an Islāmic Context*

The Islāmic context for the practice of Christian theology is perhaps unique, as it was formed largely in the Graeco-Aramaic milieu of which early Christianity was a part. Moreover, this milieu itself was largely shaped by Christianity in the period immediately prior to the rise of Islām. There is discernible Christian influence in the development of what is known as Islāmic culture or Islāmic civilization. Eastern Christians were involved in bringing to the Muslims the Greek philosophy and science which formed the core of classical Muslim civilization. In addition, Christians were prominent in letters, in medicine and even in administration—at least in the early days of Islām. This shared cultural origin and the experience of living cheek-by-jowl for thirteen hundred years has resulted in a great deal of similarity existing alongside diversity in both culture and theology.[1] It is with these elements of similarity and diversity in mind that we approach the question of developing a Christian doctrine of God within an Islāmic context.

It is important to understand the origin and development of the Muslim concept of God. In pre-Islāmic Arabia, there was knowledge of a high-god who was known as *Allāh*. Bell offers two alternatives as to how the Arabs came to a knowledge of such a god: first the *Amphictyony* theory. Each tribe is originally thought to have had its own god who would have been commonly referred to

---

*Prepared for a conference on Muslim–Chrisian relations.

as the god (*Al-ilah*). The nomadic character of the tribes often brought them together, and as part of the cultural exchange which occurred at such meetings the tribal god (*Al-ilah*) of each tribe came to be regarded as the universal God (*Allāh*) of all the tribes. Another possibility is that the pagan Arabs learned of a Supreme Deity from the followers of the monotheistic religions i.e., Jews and Christians. There is some etymological evidence to suggest that there was Syrian Christian influence.[2] The third possibility is that the notion of a high-god may have been native to the Arab tribes, and from this came the concept of a common high-god. It has been established that there is often a notion of a high-god (however neglected) in many religious traditions originally thought of as polytheistic or animistic, and it is quite possible that the notion of *Allāh* may indeed belong to Arab religion and not necessarily be an import. Development of such a concept, however, may have taken place in a situation where external stimulus was an important factor.[3]

Apart from one or two references in pre-Islāmic poetry, *Allāh* seems to have been an ignored deity. It was the vigorous preaching of the Arabian Prophet which turned the tables on the Arab gods. *Muḥammad,* whose formation was certainly influenced by Christianity and Judaism (though it also included other elements), rejected all the other popular gods of the Arabs (including the so-called 'daughters' of *Allāh*) and tirelessly preached the oneness, uniqueness and utter otherness of *Allāh. Maulānā Abū Aʿla Maudūdī* asserts that the doctrine of *Tauḥīd,* of God's absolute unity and uniqueness, is the bedrock of Islām. He goes on to outline the essentials of the Muslim doctrine of God:

> 'We have found that divinity does not vest in any material or human element of the universe, and that none of them possess even the slightest trace of it. This very inquiry leads us to the conclusion that there is a Supreme Being, over and above all that our unwary eyes see in the universe, who possesses the Divine Attributes, who is the Will behind all phenomena, the Creator of this grand universe, the Controller of its supreme law, the Governor of its serene rhythm, the Administrator of all its workings. He is *Allāh*, the Lord of the universe and has none as associate in his Divinity.'[4]

The Islāmic doctrine of God emphasizes the unity and transcendence of God. Although it is often allowed that Man has some natural knowledge of God, the doctrine of *Tauḥīd* is regarded as revealed and must be accepted *bilā kaif* (without asking how).[5] Although the monotheism of the *Qur'ān* is regarded as a definite departure from the belief of the *Jāhiliyya* (or time of barbarism), it is not regarded as a novelty but as continuous with and a development of the Judaeo-Christian biblical tradition. It may be that (initially at least), *Muḥammad* regarded himself simply as an interpreter to the Arabs of the Judaeo-Christian tradition. There are passages in the *Qur'ān* which stress the Arab character of the revelation given to *Muḥammad* (e.g. 42:7), but these have to be read with the *Qur'ānic* affirmation that God's character (*Sunnah*) does not change (35:43), as well as with the explicit claim to continuity with the biblical tradition:

> 'We believe in *Allāh* and that which was sent down to us and that which was sent down to Abraham, Ishmael, Isaac, Jacob and the tribes of Israel and that which was given to Moses and to Jesus and that which was given to all the Prophets from their Lord. We do not discriminate between any of them and to Him (i.e. *Allāh*) we have surrendered (2:136).'[6]

The *Qur'ān* claims finality but does so in the context of the wider claim that it is the climax to the older revelations. These stand abrogated (2:106) because the *Qur'ān* includes as well as fulfills them (5:13–21,51). This view has an interesting consequence since it compels Muslim scholars to reject any consideration of the literary dependence of the *Qur'ān* on the Old and New Testaments, as well as on other Jewish and Christian documents. As far as they are concerned, that which is superior cannot depend on that which is inferior. If there are points of agreement between the Jewish or Christian Scriptures, then that is only because both are revelations of God.

The claim to continuity has, however, been challenged both in ancient times and more recently. Byzantium was the nearest Christian civilization to the Islāmic world, and it is not surprising that a polemical literature about Islām developed there. The Byzantines understood the *Qur'ānic* description of *Allāh* as *Aṣ-Ṣamad (Sūrah 112)* as meaning that God was spherical *(holosphairos* or *holosphuras*). Such a belief was understandably ridiculed by them. It was a common feature of ancient Christian polemical writing to deny that *Allāh* was in any way identical with the biblical God. There were Christians within the Islāmic world who had a different approach and whose writings suggest an implicit recognition that the Muslim and the Christian are talking about the same God. St. John of Damascus (7th – 8th Century AD), is one such example. His family were prominent during the *Ummayyad* Caliphate and indeed had held high offices under the Caliph. John is sceptical about the claims to prophecy made in Islām, nevertheless, he is concerned to be fair and translates the relevant verse in *Sūrah* 112 as God the Creator of All (vs. 2).

John devotes part of his work on heresies to 'the heresy of the Ishmaelites'. In addition, his *Disputations against the Saracens* have also survived. In these works he refutes what he considers to be Muslim objections to Christian doctrines but from a standpoint which assumes a certain commonality between Christian and Muslim views of God.[7] An example is the discussion on the divinity of Christ. Muslims accuse Christians of *Shirk* (of associating partners with God) when they speak of Christ as divine. But, says John, the *Qur'ān* speaks of Christ as God's Word and Spirit. Both of these must be considered eternal since God without Word and Spirit is inconceivable. Furthermore, if they are eternal, they must be God since there cannot be another eternal besides God. The Christians are not, therefore, associating Christ with God, since he is shown to belong to the nature of God eternally; rather it is the Muslims who are mutilating (*qaṭᶜ*) God by separating from him his eternal Word and Spirit![8]

The Nestorian patriarch Timothy (8th – 9th century AD) in his famous dialogues with the *Caliph Al-Mahdī* similarly assumes that the Muslim and Christian are referring to the same God, although they understand his nature and attributes differently.

There were individual Christians in Western Christendom too who tried to relate positively to Islām: Raymond Lull advocated a peaceful approach to Islām instead of the Crusades; Francis of Assisi actually visited Saladin during the Crusades and John Wycliffe refused to deny the beatific vision to Muslims.

In modern times, the claim to continuity has been especially challenged by those who sympathize with the missiological thought of Hendrick Kraemer. Kraemer held that the Christian Gospel is unique as God's self-disclosure in a final and definitive manner. The other religions of the world are the inventions of fallen humankind and are inevitably vitiated by the total depravity of human beings. They are guilty of the sin of pride insofar as they claim to understand the nature of ultimate reality through human effort and are not willing to realize the necessity for grace.[9]

Those who would emphasize discontinuity between Islām and Christianity focus especially on the doctrine of God as found in the two systems. The Muslim doctrine of God is seen by them as 'theistic', as emphasizing the trancendence and omnipotence of God, whereas the Christian doctrine of God is seen as 'trinitarian' and 'incarnational', i.e., disclosing God in terms of loving, suffering and serving. This fundamental difference in their understanding of God has a pervasive influence in other areas as well. The virtue of humility, for example, is extolled in both faiths but the basis for humility in Islām is the glory and might of *Allāh* and the utter wretchedness of the human condition, whereas in the Christian faith true humility has its origins in the sacrificial humility of God himself. This latter is an idea totally alien to Islām.[10]

Nevertheless, many of the theologians who argue for the thesis that the Islāmic doctrine of God is discontinuous with the Judaeo-Christian tradition, allow that the Muslim concept of God is sublime and should evoke our admiration, but not our agreement. Ultimately, for them the Muslim concept of God is the product of human thought and experience and therefore 'a conceptual idol'.

The fundamental issue at stake is the nature of religious experience. Some alleged religious experience in all traditions is indubitably fake, but it is generally agreed that some religious experience in other religious traditions is genuine. How is such experience evaluated? The usual answer is that non-Christian religious traditions have access to some knowledge of God through natural revelation and conscience and that this forms the basis of their religious systems. Rudvin uses biblical theological evidence to arrive at a different conclusion. Saint Paul and the Reformers teach that man has a spark of knowledge of God's will, but it is distorted by man's fallen nature such that it is impossible to attain knowledge of salvation in this way.[11] Islām, moreover, claims to have a special revelation which is regarded as final and definitive. To arrive at an evaluation of religious experience in the Muslim context, this element must be kept in mind. For Rudvin, the alleged revelation in Islām is quite contrary to the Gospel of incarnation and atonement. This makes it impossible for him to arrive at an estimate of the doctrine of God in Islām which recognizes continuity between it and the biblical doctrine.[12] Kenneth Cragg on the other hand, while recognizing that Islām and Christianity have different views of God, can still argue for a certain amount of continuity. In 'God-talk', as far as Cragg is concerned, the subject is always the same but the predicates used of God may, and do, differ widely. In dialogue between Christians and Muslims, this becomes apparent when each party finds that it can affirm some of the attributes of God asserted by the other while disagreeing about others. Cragg admits that this disparity affects the subject, but that it is disparity regarding the one subject is, for him, obvious.[13] The question here is: at what point does disparity in predicates used of apparently the same subject lead to the recognition that the subject may not be the same?

A simple illustration may be used here: it is often found that when two people discuss a third person, there is similarity as well as disparity in predication. When the similarity outweighs the disparity it is agreed that both parties are discussing the same subject. But sometimes the disparity is so obvious that it is concluded that the two parties are not referring to the same person at all. In 'God-talk' then, at what point can we say that the disparity between descriptions of God in two different religious traditions is so great that they do not refer to the same subject? This is the fundamental issue between Cragg and Rudvin. For Cragg the similarity outweighs the disparity, whereas for Rudvin the disparity clearly outweighs the similarity. This problem is not new. Within the Christian tradition it was faced as early as the second century when Marcion rejected the Old Testament on the grounds that the God revealed in the Old Testament is vastly dissimilar to the God and Father revealed in Jesus Christ. The orthodox response was to reiterate the similarity between Old Testament and New Testament descriptions of God, while at the same time acknowledging that the revelation in Christ is fuller.

Muslims who come to Christian faith rarely reject the whole of their previous religious experience. Continuity and discontinuity are recognized. Many claim that their experience as Muslims was a preparation for their reception of the Gospel. Some claim that the incentive to consider the claims of the Gospel came from within their Islāmic milieu. At the same time, it is recognized that the Gospel judges aspects of Islām, as it does of all other systems.

The crux of the matter is the centrality of the Incarnation. If God can be known, more or less adequately, in other ways, what is the need for the Incarnation? Christians have claimed through the ages that the Incarnation is the supreme revelation to men of who God is—without it, salvific knowledge of God is not possible.

Luther asserts that God is hidden (*deus absconditus*) and inaccessible, veiled in utter darkness and yet revealed in the crib and on the cross (*deus pro nobis*). Luther claims knowledge of no other God but the one made flesh and crucified.[14]

Vis à vis Islām, two problems immediately come to the fore. Islām not only believes in the hiddenness of God, but, more seriously, in the impossibility of ever knowing him. Believers can only know his will which he has revealed to them.[15] Secondly, Islām has no conception of a suffering God, whereas the central Christian doctrines of the Incarnation and the Atonement stress that God's nature is revealed in the events of Christmas and of Good Friday as suffering love. Indeed, there is some consciousness of the suffering of God in the Old Testament, but it is in the Incarnation and the Atonement that this is defined and focused. In Asian theology today and also in much theology emerging out of Africa and Latin America, it is precisely this understanding of a suffering God which has become central to the hermeneutical and theological enterprise of getting the two horizons of Bible and culture to meet. It is because Jesus Christ shared in human suffering that the Church (as his embodiment) feels it imperative to share in human suffering today. It is because Christ redeems and liberates human beings from suffering that the Church seeks to carry forward this mission of redemption and liberation; it is because Christ pointed to the poor, the hungry, the unemployed and the imprisoned as the focus for his presence that the Church in humble service to such people seeks to meet her Lord. Without the doctrines of the Incarnation and the Atonement, such a theology of suffering would not be tenable.

Is there a way out of the impasse between Christianity and Islām? Kenneth Cragg tries to find a meeting-point in the Muslim idea of *rasūliyyah* or 'sentness'. Both Muslims and Christians believe that God has sent Prophets (*Rasūl* in fact stands for a special kind of Prophet in Islām, one to whom a book has been revealed. There are generally only four *rusul* recognized in Islām: Moses, David, Jesus and *Muḥammad*). Now, according to Cragg, 'He who sends', is somehow 'associated' with those whom he sends (Cragg is using deliberately provocative language here as both divine indwelling and association with the divine are regarded as blasphemous in orthodox Islām). The *Qur'ān* speaks of the Prophets and other believers as aided by the Holy Spirit (*Rūḥ Al-Quds;* 2:87, 253; 58:22). For Cragg belief in the 'sentness' of the Prophets and in the aid of the Holy Spirit means that the Muslim acknowledges God's special 'presence' in the revelation through the Prophets and Apostles, and in the community of believers which such a revelation brings into existence. The ethical imperative in Islām also argues for divine involvement in the human.[16]

Muslims, however, tend to speak of God's presence in terms of 'presence with' rather than in terms of 'presence in'. There is thus divine revelation and divine help but, strictly speaking, no divine involvement. It is true that God is spoken of as nearer to Man than his jugular vein (50:16) but when the *Qur'ān* speaks of his nearness to man it is often emphasizing God's omniscience or his readiness to hear supplication. Cragg argues that divine nearness and divine help imply exposure (vulnerability is the term he employs) and involvement. This may be so but it is a conclusion that Islām itself has consistently refused to draw.

From the Christian point of view, it might be said that the Christian faith draws a sharp distinction between revelation *through* the Prophets and revelation *in* the Son. The former is regarded as relative, fragmentary and obscure, whereas the latter is seen as final, definitive and complete:

> 'The revelation through the Prophets is fragmentary precisely because divine distance is maintained: in the Incarnation it is definitive precisely because this distance has been overcome. The divine is not only present with but present in. Divine involvement is complete. The paradox at the heart of the Gospel is that the sender is also the one who is sent. It is this paradox which the Muslim rejects as an antinomy.'[17]

Just as Islām refuses to recognize the humanity of God, it also refuses to countenance the teaching in Scripture and in the Fathers of the divinization of human beings.[18] The divine-human divide is quite strictly maintained and the 'inter-penetration of the divine and the human' (Cragg's phrase), which is characteristic of Scripture, is categorically rejected.

Such is the situation in orthodox Islām and, of course, it has consequences in other areas of belief. It is commonplace, for example, to hold that the Islāmic doctrine of *Tanzīh* (God's transcendence and absoluteness) has had a direct effect on the Muslim view of humanity. Even Muslim scholars allow that the traditional Muslim view of humanity has been fatalistic, although the cause is not always traced back to a particular doctrine of God.[19] The controversy between those who emphasized pre-destination and those who emphasized freedom has had as long and varied a history in Islām as in Christianity. Suffice it to say that the doctrine of *Iktisāb* (or Acquisition), which ultimately prevailed, taught that the action of a creature is created or produced by *Allāh*, but that it is acquired (*maksūb*) by the creature. The creature is simply the locus of the action and has no part in the creation of the action. The *Ashʿarites* who promoted this view were finally successful in getting the *Muʿtazilite* (or free-will) point of view suppressed, and it was not until modern times that the defence of free-will was resumed in Islām. Although the theological position of the *Ashʿarites* was sophisticated enough to allow man at least a semblance of freedom, in popular Islām even this disappeared and was replaced by the kind of fatalism represented by the words *Qismet* or *Taqdīr*.

Such an extreme view of transcendence was bound to have a reaction and this is found in *Ṣūfīsm* or Islāmic mysticism. *Ṣūfīsm* developed as a result of stimulus which Muslims received from the Christian monasticism of the Middle-East.[20] There are, broadly, two aspects of the *Ṣūfī* attempt to overcome the divine-human divide:- the first is the attempt to find the location of divinity either in the Prophet or in some *Ṣūfī* saint. The doctrine of Divine Indwelling or *Ḥulūl* was developed to make this kind of language possible. *Muḥammad* was regarded as the lamp of which *Allāh* is the flame, and divine names were ascribed to him. The doctrine of the *Haqīqat Al-Muḥammadiyya* or the created *Logos* was developed so that the Prophet could be presented as a sort of Arian Christ, and traditions which referred to *Muḥammad's* pre-existence began to be circulated.

The gradual divinization of *Muḥammad* is not restricted to *Ṣūfī* Islām but is to be found in all manifestations of popular Islām. Not only the Prophet but *Ṣūfī* adepts or guides (*murshid* in Arabic, *pīr* in Persian) began to be seen as loci for divinity. Part of the reason for this was undoubtedly the fact that, under the influence of Neo-Platonism and possibly Indian thought as well, *Ṣūfīsm* came to be dominated by the doctrine of *Waḥdat Al-Wajūd* or Monism. This led many *Ṣūfīs* to claim that they were identical with the divine Absolute. Their followers, however, often understood this as a claim to divine indwelling.[22] The *Ṣūfī* attempt at the 'self-realization' of one's own divinity is the other strand in the effort to overcome the divine-human divide.

Neo-Platonism was influential in the development of theology as well as mysticism, and it was here that the absence of the *Logos* principle in Islām was acutely felt. Some theologians at this stage indicated their willingness to accept Jesus Christ as the manifestation of the *Logos*, but quite quickly the whole *Logos*-terminology, in a slightly reduced form, was transferred to *Muḥammad*.[23]

The tendency in Islām to divinize the Prophet or some other figure is symptomatic of a felt need. The Indian poet, *ʿAllama Sir Muḥammad Iqbāl* sums it up in the following lines of *Payām-i-Mashriq*:

> 'The eye cannot contain him, said wisdom,
> (yet) the glance of desire is in hope and fear,
> The story of Sinai does not grow old,
> The desire of Moses is in every heart.'[24]

This brings us back to the importance of the doctrine of the Incarnation in a Muslim context.

Islām and Christianity both acknowledge the importance of history. The historicity of the Jesus-event is, therefore, critically important in the Muslim context, and also that of Salvation History as recorded in the Scriptures. There is a fashion in some current theological thinking in Asia to denigrate Salvation History and to shy away from the 'scandal of particularity'. Against this it has rightly been emphasized that biblical Salvation History is normative for us as Christians and is the means whereby we determine what it is that constitutes 'salvation histories' in our varying religio-cultural contexts. It is the Bible which guides us in our assessment of what is 'authentically preparatory' in the other traditions. A defence of the historicity of Salvation History leads us necessarily to a defence of the integrity of Scripture.[25] Salvation History, of course, is to be seen not only as a particular interpretation of history but as the history of God's decisive intervention in human affairs. It is on such a view of biblical history that the whole of our Soteriology depends. Islām, of course, accepts divine intervention, but not the kind of intensely personal intervention which the Incarnation proclaims. This is the issue between Muslims and Christians: how closely, personally and sacrificially is God involved in human affairs? Is he to be seen as the Sovereign who commands? or is he also to be seen as suffering, self-giving love, inviting man's free response to this unmerited favour?

> 'That which was from the beginning, which we have heard, which we have seen with our eyes, which we have looked at and our hands have touched—this we proclaim concerning the Word of Life. The life appeared; we have seen it and testify to it, and we proclaim to you the Eternal Life, which was with the Father and has appeared to us' (1 John 1:1–2).

Deo Gratias!

CHAPTER 2

Christology in an Islāmic Context*

Introduction

Christology in an Islāmic context is not the same as an Islāmic Christology. The latter would be a specifically Muslim view of Christ,[1] whereas the former is a Christian Christology developed within a Muslim socio-cultural situation and addressed to it.

Radical and Orthodox approaches

The person of our Lord has been of late the subject of much controversy between professional theologians in the West. The more 'radical' have so overstressed his humanity that they have either neglected or, in some cases, denied his divinity and, as a necessary consequence, any notion of his Incarnation. Their views are little different from the orthodox Muslim view of the person of Jesus Christ. Muslims rightly claim affinity between their own view and that of these 'radical' theologians.

The 'orthodox' reply to these theologians has been of a high order but has often been couched in the traditional language of Christian theology and is, therefore, opaque to the Muslim. Also, the reply often takes the form of an exploration into the terms used

*The paper first appeared in *Sharing Jesus in the Two-Thirds World* edied by Samuel and Sugden, PIM/Eerdmans 1984.

in the New Testament. Although this is a valid procedure within the confines of the Christian Church, it can only be used with great reserve with the Muslim as he is not convinced of the authenticity of the New Testament. The ancient Christian Churches of the Islāmic East have generally confined themselves to reaffirming traditional Christological doctrine whether in its Chalcedonian or non-Chalcedonian form.

Is a more dynamic approach possible?

I THE PERSON OF CHRIST

The whole question of the person of Christ is intimately linked to the doctrine of the Trinity: if Christ is God and the Holy Spirit is also God, why are there not three gods but only one God? The traditional answer that there are three persons who all share the one substance of the Godhead is not easily understood by the Muslim. For him God's individuality is absolutely unique and brooks no plurality, certainly no plurality of persons.[2] The ordinary word for person in Arabic and some other Islāmic languages is *Shakhṣ* which carries with it connotations of psychological autonomy. This makes it difficult to speak of three persons and one God at the same time. Augustine himself used the word person in this context with great reserve and only because he considered it better than keeping silent on the issue. The Latin *persona* was a translation of the Greek *prosōpon* which means face or aspect and even as little as an actor's mask. The exact Arabic equivalent is *Shakl* which means a form, aspect, figure or mode. The traditional Eastern Christian word for a Person of the Blessed Trinity is *Aqnūm* (pl. *Aqānīm*). This is the exact equivalent of *hypostasis* and can, in other contexts, mean 'constitutive element'. When Muslim commentators like *Al-Ṭabarī* discuss the Christian doctrine of the Trinity they often use this last term.[3]

Modalism

Those who have attempted to articulate a more or less conservative Christology within an Islāmic context have often tried to do so in two major ways.

One group begins with a consideration of the Trinity. After rightly rejecting the error that the persons of the Trinity are in some way persons in the modern psychological sense, they conclude that the only alternative is some kind of modalism. The temptation to come to this conclusion is strong as the *Qur'ān* itself speaks of God manifesting himself in different ways, e.g. in the burning bush to Moses (20:10f.). *Ṣūfī* tradition also talks of God's many modes (*Gūna*) of revelation.[4] The temptation is to translate *prosōpon* by *Shakl* and to speak of God as manifesting himself in different modes or *Ashkāl*. Jesus Christ then becomes the particular manifestation (*Tajallī*) of God at that particular time. This is the doctrine of *Tropos apokalupseos* or of the Trinity of manifestation and is most associated with the name of Sabellius (3rd century AD). The different modes of the Trinity are regarded as successive and the problem arises as to which, if any, of the modes reflects the nature of God as he is in himself? If the 'hidden' God has manifested himself in these ways, none of which necessarily reveal his essential self, what advantage has the Christian doctrine of God over the Islāmic doctrine? For that also teaches that God manifests and reveals his will but remains hidden in himself. Furthermore, why should there be only these manifestations of God? Is he not free to manifest himself, as the *Ṣūfīs* claim, in a hundred thousand different ways? If any kind of modalism is permissible, it must regard the different 'modes' of the Trinity as modes of being, as 'aspects' perhaps but not successive manifestations. The aspects must be seen as 'constitutive elements' of the being of God, as permanent rather than passing, as revealing God as he is in himself. If the word *Ashkāl* is to be used of such modes it must be clearly understood that these *Ashkāl* of God are co-existent aspects or faces of God and are not successive. It may be, however, that in the economy of salvation they are successively *revealed*.

Nestorianism

The second group begins with the person of Christ. After rightly claiming that one must have both Christ's humanity and his divinity in mind, it often arrives at a radically Nestorian solution to the problem of how to explain Christ to the Muslim. Some come to this conclusion as a result of a *Qur'ānic* exegesis which insists upon solving the problem of Christology in the *Qur'ān* by claiming that wherever the divinity of Christ is denied, only the human Jesus is meant, whereas wherever it is affirmed the indwelling *Logos* is meant.[5] This makes for a Nestorian Christology with the two natures of Christ rigidly separated. It substitutes for the doctrine of the Incarnation, a doctrine of *Ḥulūl* or Indwelling. The consequence is that God's 'distance' from the world is maintained and his impassibility is preserved. This has some interesting results.

For example, much preaching on the passion of our Lord in Pākistān claims that only the human Jesus suffered on the cross and that the divinity abandoned him in order to preserve its impassibility. This is the commonest exegesis, in certain circles, of the cry of dereliction. Christians thus tend to lose sight of the important truth that God has, in Christ, suffered for us, that he has given up his transcendence and omnipotence in order that he might identify himself with us in our weakness, poverty and death. Certainly, Christ has two natures but they are such a close union that they may also be spoken of as one. The humanity has been taken up into his divinity. Whatever happens to the human nature also affects the divine *Logos*. This is why Ignatius, for example, can speak of the 'passion of our God'.[6]

Much recent theology rightly takes God's involvement with man, as supremely manifested in the Incarnation, as a point of departure for making a case for Christian involvement with the poor, the deprived, the sick, and the oppressed.[7] Such an argument is impossible on the Nestorian view of the nature of Christ since here God's presence is half-hearted at best and does not in any way involve a *kenōsis* (or self-emptying. Cf. Phil. 2:7).

To put forward a Nestorian view in an Islāmic context may buy us cheap approval for a while. But it does not come to grips with the fundamental issue between Islām and Christianity that God has become flesh and dwelt amongst us. Strictly speaking, the Islāmic God can be merciful but he cannot be compassionate. He cannot share our suffering because he has never been incarnate. *Iqbāl* tries to articulate the dilemma of the sensitive Muslim in this regard:

> 'God is beyond death and is the essence of life,
> God does not know what the death of man is,
> Though we be as naked birds,
> In the knowledge of death we are better than God!'[8]

This is the logical result of believing in an utterly transcendent and impassible God. It would not apply to the Christian idea of God who tastes suffering and death in the person of Jesus Christ, where the humanity of Jesus Christ is so closely united to his divinity that what happens to the one can be said to happen to the other.

Dā'ūd Rahbar, in a letter to his friends explaining why he has become a Christian, argues that the *Qur'ānic* doctrine of God's justice demands that such a God be himself involved in suffering and be seen as involved in suffering. Only then can he be a just judge of suffering humanity. A God that is preserved from suffering will be an arbitrary and capricious judge. *Dā'ūd* believes that God's suffering is focused supremely in the birth, life and death of Jesus of Nazareth. It is here that God's involvement with humanity reaches a climax and that God's justice is seen as love. God's presence in the innocent suffering of Jesus 'for righteousness' sake' justifies and redeems humanity.

Generation or Procession?

One of the doctrines regarding the person of Christ which Muslims find most offensive is that he is the only-begotten Son of God. *Sūrah* 112 of the *Qur'ān* makes it clear that God neither begets nor is begotten. It has been suggested that this *Sūrah* was originally directed against the pagan Arab belief in the daughters of *Allāh* as intercessors with *Allāh*. It has also been suggested that this *Sūrah* is directed primarily against the teaching of St. Cyril of Jerusalem which was widely known among the Christians of Arabia.[9]

Whatever the original intention of this *Sūrah*, it inculcated a prejudice in the Muslim mind regarding language which associates generation with God. In the Muslim mind the generation of the Son often means his birth of the Virgin Mary. Christians often encouraged this error themselves. For example, when *Muḥammad* denied the Sonship of Christ in the presence of the Christians of *Najrān*, they are reputed to have asked him who Jesus' father was —clearly referring to his earthly birth. Some Christian literature published in the Middle-East claims that Jesus is Son of God, because he had no human father. And yet whenever the early Fathers refer to the generation of the Son they mean his 'eternal Birth'. They nearly always referred to the earthly birth as the Incarnation. It is a moot point whether the ecumenical councils and the Fathers were mistaken in using the expression, 'the eternal birth'. Could, for example, the fact that 'time' was often seen as coming into being with creation have led to the view that the expression 'the Son was born eternally' meant that he was created before our 'time' but one could, nevertheless, picture the Father at first without the Son and then picture the Son coming into being. It is clear that this view was taken in some circles. Nevertheless when most of the early writers spoke of the Son's 'eternal birth' they meant that the Father was the source of being and that the Son proceeded from the Father. The Father, then, was the *ratio essendi* of the Son. The doctrine of the Eternal Generation was concerned to show that the relation between the Father and the Son was analogous to the logical relation between ground and consequent.

We may agree that the Fathers and the councils were using and, to some extent, were bound by the very inadequate categories of Hellenistic metaphysics. For example, many of the Fathers tried to 'save' the Hellenistic doctrine of the Impassibility of God despite the early conviction that God had been involved in human suffering in the Incarnation. Again, the generation of the Son was sometimes interpreted in Neo-Platonic emanationist terms which tended to hold that the generation of the *Logos* preserved the essential isolation of the One. We must, however, view the dilemma of the early Church in sympathetic terms. The Fathers were grappling with realities which challenged all the old presuppositions and at the same time demanded a response. Quite often the response was in the form of paradox.

For example, Ignatius (d. 108 AD) in a famous passage in his *Epistle to the Ephesians* tries to articulate certain aspects of the paradox in this way:

> There is one Physician, of flesh and of spirit, originate and unoriginate, God in man, true life in death, Son of Mary and Son of God, first passible and then impassible, Jesus Christ our Lord.[10]

Ignatius refers to Christ as both *agennētos* and as *gennētos* i.e. as both ungenerate and as generate. He recognizes that to speak of the generation of the Son is only a metaphorical way of referring to the Father as the Ground of Being of the Son. The Son could equally be called ungenerate as he has no beginning in time. In this connection Ignatius speaks of the Son 'proceeding' (*proelthonta*) from the Father. Later on he refers to Christ as, 'His Word, coming forth from silence . . .'[11] Tradition has always considered Ignatius to have been a disciple of St. John. It is therefore interesting to see that John also speaks of Christ as proceeding (*exēlthon*) from God (Jn. 8:42).

In our Islāmic context it may be worth stressing this aspect of 'procession' (which could be translated by *Ṣadara* in the way the procession of the Spirit is) over and against the language of generation. *Qur'ānic* Christology, such as it is, lends itself much more to 'processional' than to generational language. We must use the *Qur'ānic* titles of Jesus with great reserve as Muslims invariably ascribe similar, if not higher, titles to *Muḥammad*. When, however, we declare Jesus to be the Word of God or the Truth or his Spirit, we are using terms which a Muslim cannot deny though he may qualify them. Such terms, therefore, often make a useful point of departure for talking to the Muslim about the person of Christ.[12]

Most of the titles used of Jesus in the *Qur'an* are susceptible of a processional interpretation. We shall give detailed consideration to three of these.

The Sent One

He is referred to as *'Rasūl'* (4:171) or 'the Sent One.' This is paralleled in the very passage in John where Jesus refers to himself as proceeding from the Father (Jn. 8:16, 29).

For the Muslim, a *Rasūl* is a special kind of Prophet to whom a book has been vouchsafed. There are, generally speaking, only four *Rusul* recognized by Islām: Moses, David, Jesus and *Muḥammad.* As has been pointed out earlier, Bishop Cragg, in a very original but neglected article,[13] has tried to show that the Muslim idea of *rasūliyyah* or 'sentness' can be developed in such a way as to narrow the gap between Muslim and Christian ideas of revelation. Both Muslims and Christians believe that God has sent Prophets. The one who sends is somehow 'associated' with those whom he sends. The one who is sent is somehow full of the one who sends. The *Qur'ān* repeatedly speaks of the Prophets and other believers, as aided by the Holy Spirit (*Ruḥ Al-Quds,* 2:87, 253, where the reference is to Jesus, 58:22). For Cragg, the belief in the sending of the Prophets and in the aid of the Holy Spirit means that the Muslim acknowledges God's special 'presence' in the revelation through his Prophets and Apostles and in the community of believers which this revelation brings into existence.

Revelations with a strong ethical imperative, as Cragg believes Islām to possess, argue necessarily for divine involvement in the human. Two questions, however, remain. First, to what extent is God's presence, for the Muslim, presence *with* and not presence *in*? Orthodox Islām always maintains the human-divine divide quite strictly. It is only in *Ṣūfī* mystical speculation that this divide sometimes appears to have been overcome. Even here the identification of the divine with the human is often more apparent than real. Secondly, to what extent is the Christian distinction between revelation *through* the Prophets and revelation *in* the Son, one of kind and not simply of degree (cf. Heb. ch. 1)? Although the Christian may accept 'God's presence *with*' as a model of revelation through the Prophets, when he speaks of the Incarnation, a totally different kind of model is needed. The revelation through the prophets is fragmentary precisely because divine distance is maintained. In the Incarnation it is definitive precisely because this distance has been overcome. The divine is not only present *with* but present *in*. Divine involvement is complete. The paradox at the heart of the Gospel is that the sender is also the one who is sent. It is this paradox which the Muslim rejects as an antinomy. Much of the task of Christology in an Islāmic context lies in showing the Muslim that the Incarnation is not a contradiction in terms.

Spirit of God

He is explicitly referred to as a Spirit proceeding from God (*Rūḥ*^{un}*Min*^{hu}) in 4:171. A common Muslim title for Jesus is *Rūḥ Allāh* or Spirit of God. Whatever Christian apologists may say, the Muslim does not intend this title to ascribe divinity to Jesus. Jesus *is* a spirit from God but he is a created spirit. The *Qur'ān* refers to Jesus as a spirit proceeding from God. In sharp contrast, the New Testament refers to the Holy Spirit as the Spirit of Christ (Rom. 8:9, Acts 16:7). Whether or not this argues for a double-procession of the Spirit, as the Western Church would have it, it is at least certain that the Spirit is *given to the Church* by Christ.

The Word of God

He is called the Word of God (4:171) and (possibly) the Word of Truth (19:34), i.e. the Word which proceeds from God. It is around this phrase that controversy is centred. In 4:171 Jesus is called the *Kalima* of God. The ancient Christian apologists like John of Damascus and Timothy of Baghdād understood this to mean that Jesus was being identified with the eternal Word of God in the *Qur'ān*. They used this as an argument to show the divinity of Jesus Christ as follows. Muslims believe that God has no partners or equals. Nothing can, therefore, be eternal but God alone. But Muslims also believe the Word of God to be eternal. Therefore, the Word of God must be God. Jesus is called the Word of God in the *Qur'ān*, therefore Jesus must be God.

John of Damascus says, for example, that if Christians are accused by the Muslims of *Shirk* (of ascribing partners with God) the Muslims may rightly, if the *Qur'ān* be true, be accused of mutilating (*qaṭʿ*) God by separating from him his Word and Spirit.[14]

Also, in Arabic usage the phrase *Kalimatullāh* is used of the Scriptures which the Muslims believe to be the eternal speech of God.[15]

In recent years, however, modern scholars of Islām and of Arabic have claimed that *Kalima* means the ordinary, created words (such as commands) of God and may not be confused with the eternal Word of God, for which they would use the word *Kalām*. They would equate *Kalima* with *rhēma* which they would take to mean the individual, contingent words of God. They would equate *Kalām* with *Logos* which they would take to mean the eternal Word of God. Whether there is an exact equivalent to *logos* in Arabic is uncertain. But when Greek philosophy began to influence Muslim thought, *Logos* was usually translated *Kalām*. It remains open, to my mind, whether this was not an arbitrary choice and whether *Kalima* might equally well have been chosen.

God's creative command 'Be' is his *Amr*, often called *Kalima*. This creative command is associated in the *Qur'ān* both with the birth of Jesus and with the creation of Adam.[16] Both were *de novo* events brought about by God's creative *Kalima*. The significant difference for the Christian apologist is that Adam is never identified with this creative *Kalima* of God, whereas Jesus is. In other words, we may say that whereas the divine Word brings both the human Jesus and the human Adam into being, it is only with the former that he comes to be 'associated'.

It would seem then that the Muslim would be less offended by the language of procession than by the language of generation which is completely alien to his whole tradition.

II THE WORK OF CHRIST

As far as the work of Christ is concerned, the *Qur'ān* rejects the whole idea of vicarious atonement (6:164). The Muslim translator and commentator of the *Qur'ān, Yusuf 'Ali,* says *inter alia* about 6:164:

> 'We are fully responsible for our acts ourselves: we cannot transfer the consequences to someone else. Nor can anyone vicariously atone for our sins.'[17]

But the situation is not so unambiguous. *Fuad Accad* points out one place in the *Qur'ān* where the idea of a ransom sacrifice is clearly mentioned. The passage is 37:107 and the context is Abraham's preparedness to sacrifice his own son (who is not named in the *Qur'ānic* text). The narrative in the *Qur'ān* follows the biblical account and ends with God ransoming the boy with a 'tremendous victim'. Here, the idea of one life being substituted for another is clearly present. Abraham's preparedness to sacrifice his son is still commemorated by Muslims at the *'Īd-ul-Aḍḥā* when a thanksgiving sacrifice is offered. The treatment in the *Qur'ān* of the death of Christ is ambiguous too. Some passages clearly speak of his death (19:33). Others go so far as to suggest that Jesus died according to 'the definite plan and foreknowledge of God' (3:55). The passage that has dominated Muslim thinking about the death of Christ is 4:157:

> 'that they (i.e. the Jews) said in boast: "We killed Christ Jesus the Son of Mary, the Apostle of God." But they killed him not, nor crucified him, but so it was made to appear to them and those who differ therein are full of doubts, with no knowledge, but only conjecture to follow, for of a surety they killed him not.'

Muslims traditionally believe this verse to mean that Jesus was not crucified but that either Judas or Simon of Cyrene was substituted in his place while he was taken up alive to heaven. In order to reconcile this view with other passages in the *Qur'ān* which speak of Jesus' death, Muslim commentators often adopt the view that although Jesus *was* taken up alive, his death will occur at his second coming (a belief in Jesus' Second Coming is quite common among Muslims). Some ancient Muslim commentators on the *Qur'ān* accept that Jesus died on the cross but that his body was then assumed into heaven. Certain modern sects like the *Aḥmadiyya* believe that although Jesus was crucified, he did not die on the cross but was taken down in a coma. He subsequently revived and travelled to Kashmir where he finally died a natural death. There is even a tomb in Kashmir alleged to be that of Jesus.

Both Prof. R. C. Zaehner and Prof. Geoffrey Parrinder in their exegesis of 4:157 refer to the view that the verse is not denying that Jesus was crucified but does deny that it was the Jews who crucified him. In other words, it was God himself who was ultimately responsible. This view accords well with both the *Qur'ān* (3:55) and with the New Testament (John 19:11, Acts 2:23).[18] In this connection, Parrinder remarks 'there is no futurity in the grammar of the *Qur'ān* to suggest a post-millenial death. The plain meaning seems to be his physical death at the end of his present human life on earth.'[19]

For the Christian apologist, the fact that most Muslims are reluctant to admit that Jesus died is in itself remarkable. The *Qur'ān* repeatedly accuses the Jews of killing the prophets of old (2:61, 71). It even discusses the possibility of *Muḥammad's* own death (3:144). Why then was it so impossible for Jesus (a Prophet, from the Muslim point of view) to have been crucified? Is there an implied docetic Christology here? Whatever the *Qur'ān* may say about the death of Jesus, it is clear that this death (if it is acknowledged at all) is not in any way understood as an *atoning* death, at least as far as the *Qur'ān* is concerned.

In the *Ṣūfī* or mystical tradition in Islām, Jesus is often the pattern for self-denial and sacrifice. His death is often seen as the culmination of a life of self-sacrifice. Some modern Muslims too are beginning to see the redemptive value of Jesus' suffering. Their emphasis is generally upon his willingness to suffer for righteousness' sake rather than upon the actual crucifixion itself. They see in this willingness a complete surrender to God's will and lay stress upon the constructive aspect of suffering when it is endured for God's sake.

Christ's obedience is surely the most effective way to begin talking to the Muslim about the atonement. The Muslim often understands concepts of solidarity very quickly. It may be possible to explain to him that just as we, who are Adam's progeny, share in the sinfulness which he brought into the world, so also Christ as representative man, as the Second Adam, returns us to the obedience for which we were created. He came to do what we, of our own nature, cannot do and are not inclined to do. God accepts this offering of free obedience as the human return to God's obedience and, therefore, to his favour. (This, I suppose, is more or less a reworking of the old doctrine of Acceptilation). Cardinal John Henry Newman summed all this up beautifully in his hymn, 'Praise to the Holiest in the height':

O loving wisdom of our God!
When all was sin and shame,
A second Adam to the fight
And to the rescue came.

O wisest love! that flesh and blood
Which did in Adam fail,
Should strive afresh against the foe
Should strive and should prevail.

God invites men to offer themselves to him in union with Christ. It is only through and in this representative sacrifice that any offering is accepted and any reconciliation effected. It remains true that the giver of this invitation also *enables* us to accept this invitation and that this 'enabling' is, potentially at least, for everyone.

The Resurrection

One cannot talk about the atoning death of Christ, without discussing God's seal of acceptance upon this supreme act of obedience, the resurrection. One expression that the *Qur'ān* uses for the raising of Jesus has to do with the root verb *rafa* and is rightly translated as Assumption or Ascension into heaven.[20] However, another word is used for the raising of Jesus from the dead and this is *ba'ath^a^* (19:33). This word is used of others in terms of a physical resurrection from the dead at the last day (e.g. of John the Baptist in 19:15).

The *Qur'ān,* however, does not leave Jesus dead (assuming that it does speak of his death) but speaks of his glorification immediately after his death. Most Muslims believe that Jesus was taken up body, soul and spirit into heaven. This argues for a resurrection from the dead. As far as the *Aḥmadiyya* are concerned, they do not give sufficient weight to aspects of their own Islāmic tradition, to the testimony of contemporary secular historians and to the unanimous witness of Christians down the ages regarding Christ's death on the cross. Nor do they take seriously enough the *Qur'ānic* testimony to the Glorification and bodily Assumption of Jesus into heaven.[21]

The Ethical Teaching of Christ

Christ's teaching as recorded in the Gospels is very important in the task of developing a Christian theology in the Muslim world. A theologian working in a Muslim context will, it is to be hoped, like any other theologian, take full account of textual criticism and the results obtained by it in determining the original texts. He will also be aware that it was the needs of the early Church which gave rise to our New Testament documents and they they are, to some extent, shaped by these needs. He will, however, also be aware that the early Church was not cavalier in adapting Christ's teaching to its own needs but was extremely conscientious and conservative in recording the *ipsissima vox Jesu* even where it did not fully understand it. An example might be the Son of Man sayings which are faithfully recorded in the Gospels but not much used in other early Christian writing, canonical or otherwise. In other words, his attitude must not be reductionist. At the same time he should not eschew his critical faculties. Muslims often look upon the teaching of Christ as a radical alternative to the Islāmic system. (Whether they accept or reject such an alternative is quite another matter). Of particular importance are Christ's teachings on revenge, adultery, divorce, prayer and fasting, and on the relationship between 'exterior' and 'interior' religion. In these areas the contrast between the Islāmic system and the gospel is most clearly seen. The Christian emphasis on 'change of heart', whether understood individually or socially, as opposed to a mere manipulation of structures provides a credible alternative to the enforcement of *Sharī'ah* (or Islāmic Law).

No mere metaphysical subtleties are going to win the Muslim to

Christ. Until he is confronted by the person of Christ as found in the Gospels and in the life of the Church, he will not find it possible to acknowledge Christ as Lord. The character of Christ, as Andrae points out, is immeasurably superior to any other human character[22] and the excellence of his teaching, the power of his miracles, the commitment of his obedience unto death and his glorious resurrection all conspire together to convict men and women as to who he really is.

CHAPTER 3

A Recovery of Traditional Christology in the Asian Context*

Traditional Christological doctrine claims to be a development of the biblical doctrine. The most important biblical motif in this respect is 'The Word of God' understood as God's directive and creative Word (e.g. Ps. 33:6). Already in the prophetic books 'The Word' is personally conceived (Is. 55:11, Jer. 23:29). In the *Targums* (paraphrases of the Old Testament), 'The Word' (or *Memra*) is used to speak of Yahweh without using his name. (The Aramaic *Memra* is related to Arabic *Amr* which is used in the *Qur*'ān for God's directive and creative Word).[1] In Hellenistic Judaism this concept was further developed; Philo, for example, combined the Greek and the biblical ideas in his doctrine of the *Logos* as that which creates and sustains the Universe and is a mediator between God and Man.

The New Testament doctrine is clearly influenced by these various strands of thought. What is new, however, is that the NT doctrine is about the *incarnate* Word. The coming of the Messiah is identified with the Word of God (which now means God the Word) taking flesh. There are hints even in the Old Testament that the coming of the Messiah is the coming of God himself (Isaiah 7:14, 9:6). Only in the New Testament however, is the distance between God and Man finally and decisively overcome in the incarnation of

*A background paper for a *Christian Conference of Asia*, Consultation on Christology, Chieng Mai, 1984.

God the Word.[2] Another important motif is that of 'The Son of Man' (Dan. 7:13). This title has more to do with the divine character of the coming King than with his humanity. The New Testament frequently agrees with the inter-testamental and the contemporary Jewish belief that the title refers to a glorious, divine King (cf. Matt. 25:31ff.).[3] It seems that the early Church was unaware of its significance, as it is almost never discussed in the Fathers in these terms; nor even in the canon of the NT, apart from the Gospels. Other important motifs in the Bible are the Isaianic 'Servant of Yahweh' and the coming Prophet (Deut. 18:18). The evangelists reported that the crowds interpreted Jesus' ministry in terms of this latter expectation, while Jesus himself seems to have understood it in terms of the former.

It was, however, the doctrine of the incarnate Word which caught the imagination of the early Church, and its theology was definitely one of the Incarnation. Even the doctrine of the Atonement was discussed within the context of the doctrine of the Incarnation. For example, one of the problems that was discussed quite often is how an impassible god could assume a passible nature. In contemporary Hellenistic thought, God was beyond any kind of change (the unmoved mover). The early Church was faced with the problem of explaining to such a culture the truth that God had suffered in Christ. Sometimes both the impassibility of God and his suffering are affirmed in the same statement.[4]

In the early Church, two main traditions developed regarding Christology. The school of Antioch was devoted to biblical exegesis and to an assessment of Jesus of Nazareth as presented in the Gospels. They began with the man Jesus and asked how he could be God. They were mostly practitioners of what we would call today 'a Christology from below.'[5]

The school of Alexandria approached the matter quite differently. They began with the divine *Logos* and asked how he could be spoken of as assuming humanity. They emphasized the deification of the human as much as the incarnation of the divine. We would call this 'a Christology from above.' It is in the context of the rivalry between these two schools of theology that the Christological controversies which divided the early Church are to be understood. The Antiochene school began increasingly to speak of God 'indwelling' in Jesus Christ, whereas the Alexandrian school spoke more and more of the 'union' of the two natures in the incarnate Lord. The former movement ended in 'Nestorianism', while the latter developed into 'Monophysitism'. The attempt at the Council of Chalcedon to bring them together only resulted in a third party coming into existence. The Church in the East continues to this day to be divided along these lines. The Christological controversies of the early centuries continue to find expression in three living ecclesiastical traditions.

The Chalcedonian Orthodox Churches, along with the Christian West, reaffirm the Chalcedonian definition;

> 'Following, therefore, the holy fathers, we confess one and the same Our Lord Jesus Christ, and we all teach harmoniously (that he is) the same perfect in Godhead, the same perfect in Manhood, truly God and truly Man, the same of a reasonable soul and body, consubstantial with the Father in Godhead, and the same consubstantial with us in Manhood, like us in all things except sin; begotten before ages of the Father in Godhead, the same in the last days for us and for our salvation (born) of Mary the virgin *Theotokos* (God-bearer) in manhood, one and the same Christ, Son, Lord, unique; acknowledged in two natures without confusion, without change, without division, without separation—the difference of the nature being by no means taken away because of the union, but rather the distinctive character of each nature being preserved and (each) combining in one Person and *hypostasis*—not divided or separated into two persons, but one and the same Son and only begotten God, Word, Lord Jesus Christ.'

The Chalcedonian formula affirms the two natures (*physeis*) united in one *hypostasis*.[6]

Some Oriental Orthodox believed that to speak of two natures after the Union was to maintain a kind of 'schizophrenia' in the personality of the incarnate Lord. They would allow that Jesus Christ is from or out of two natures, but that he is one nature himself. They claimed inspiration from Cyril's formula 'one nature (*mia physis*) of the Word of God incarnate.' Two *ousiai* (or substances) in the one nature of the incarnate Lord were, however, allowed. The Coptic, Jacobite and Armenian Churches are the spiritual descendants of those who refused to accept Chalcedon. They are concerned to maintain the Unity of the incarnate Lord, and speak of the one nature of God, the *Logos* incarnate, appropriating to himself a perfect, complete and real manhood. The *Logos* is regarded by them as the sole subject of which all divine and human activities of the incarnate Lord are to be predicated.

In recent times, some linguistic clarification has taken place. We now know, for example, that what the Chalcedonians mean by *physis* is denoted by *ousia* for the Non-chalcedonians. So whereas Chalcedon speaks of two natures united in one *hypostasis*, the Non-chalcedonians speak of two substances united in one nature.

The third group are Nestorians (though it is doubtful whether Nestorius himself would have qualified as one). They emphasize the difference in the natures of the incarnate Lord and speak of a union of good pleasure rather than the hypostatic union of Chalcedon. Although they speak of the two natures of Christ, they assert that it is the one Christ who is worshipped. Perhaps their position is not so very different from that of Pope Leo's *Tome* which was approved at Chalcedon; that the two natures came together into one *prosōpon* (or Person).[7] They have often been accused, however, of believing that Christ had two *prosōpa*.

The Chalcedonian (or Eastern) Orthodox and the Non-chalcedonian (or Oriental) Orthodox have recently produced a series of agreements on Christological questions under the auspices of the World Council of Churches, and there is a real possibility of restored communion between them.[8] The Nestorians (The Church of the East) were excluded from the discussions but the report expresses the hope that further linguistic and doctrinal clarification will allow discussions to begin even with them.[9]

The belief expressed by Bar Hebraeus in the thirteenth century and quoted by Archbishop Severius during the above-mentioned discussions may become the basis of Christian unity in the east. Bar Hebraeus is reported to have said, 'I am convinced that the dispute of Christians among themselves is not based on essentials, but on words and terms. For all Christians confess that Christ is perfect God and perfect man without mixture or confusion of natures. While one refers to the union of natures as "nature", another calls it "Person" and a third "*prosōpon*". Thus I see that all Christians, though they remain separate are, in fact, in agreement.'[10]

The real issue in the Christological controversies, was whether God was involved in the suffering of Christ. Both the followers of Cyril and the Chalcedonians agreed that God was fully involved in Christ's suffering. Cyril's followers often quoted his demand that Nestorius should acknowledge that 'The Word of God suffered in the flesh.'[11] On the Chalcedonian side the *Tome of Leo* is quite clear: '. . . the only begotten Son of God was crucified and buried' in accordance with that saying of the Apostle 'for had they known they would not have crucified the Lord of Majesty'.[12] The insertion of the words 'Who was crucified for us' in the *Trisagion* makes liturgical use of the same idea. Nestorius and his followers were accused of believing that it was only the man Jesus who suffered, the impassible *Logos* remaining untouched by this suffering. The apologies of the Nestorian Patriarch Timothy of Baghdād are ambiguous in this respect. Sometimes they seem to affirm that the Word suffered due to union with the body, while at other times they deny that the indwelling *Logos* suffered.[13]

The Christology of the early Church was rooted in the masses.[14] It was what today would be called 'a people's theology' and as such it produced a whole corpus of devotional literature.[15] There is a tendency to regard the Christological controversies of the early centuries as so much hair-splitting by professional theologians and to ignore their deep roots in the psychology of the masses. One of the reasons why Nestorius was so unpopular was his denial of the title *Theotokos* to the Blessed Virgin, a title she already possessed in popular devotion. His separation of the human and divine in the Person of Christ implied that the body of Christ received in the Eucharist was not divine and, therefore, not 'the medicine of immortality' it had been believed to be since the time of Ignatius.[16]

Early Christological thinking was constructive: the minimum requirements were given and the parameters set but further thought was encouraged. There was not the constant re-examination of roots which has made much modern Christology radical but unconstructive. Analysis of Scripture and of the Fathers was profound but this was succeeded by creative, synthetic thought. In the course of time, however, the definitions of the councils become formulae to be recited rather than stimulants to further thought. The other side of such a popularly-based theology was a great deal of intolerance of other opinions: the judgement of heresy was made too hastily, popular errors began to be given official theological sanction, local crowds usually supported their own theologians, heightening the dangers of schism.

Early Christological doctrines were developed in a pluralist environment, particularly in an environment of classical paganism (though Christianity was present in other environments, such as the Ethiopian or the Persian). Christianity had a dialectical relationship with classical paganism; whilst Christians were opposed to popular forms of paganism and 'vain philosophy', they used the methods of Hellenistic philosophy to develop their own theology and thus confute paganism. This relationship is analogous to that which developed between Islāmic theology and Hellenistic philosophy later on, as, for example, in the works by *Al-Ghazālī*.[17] With the Nestorian advance into India and China came contact with Buddhism, Hindūism and Confucianism. Christianity returned to its early state of secular powerlessness in the Middle East with the rise of Islām.

The contribution to Christian theology by Christians living in the Islāmic Empire is a significant one. John of Damascus' *De Fide Orthodoxa* is an important exercise in systematic theology and has greatly influenced subsequent Christian theology as well as the development of *Kalām* or formal theology in Islām.[18] His dialogues with a Muslim interlocutor are well known, and have been discussed elsewhere.[19] Timothy of Baghdād's dialogues with the *Caliph Al-Mahdī* are also quite well known and continue to make a useful contribution to Muslim-Christian discussion.[20] Other Christians like *Ḥunain bin Isḥāq* made important contributions to learning. The contribution made by Christians to the development of an intellectual tradition in the Islāmic world should be a source of inspiration to Christians living in the Muslim world today.[21]

What then is the precise relevance of our exercise in attempting to recover the traditional Christology of the Eastern Churches? First, we saw that traditional Christology is a theology of the incarnation. In modern Christology we often face a dilemma; on the one hand we have progressive theologians (including many Asians), stressing the involvement of God with the pain of the world.[22] They do not restrict their theology to the Incarnation and the cross (they are quite aware, for example, that there is an understanding of this suffering of God in the Prophets). The Incarnation and the cross are, however, seen as the focus and supreme example of God's involvement with the world. On the other hand, 'radical' theologians challenge the doctrine of the Incarnation and so the very basis of progressive, incarnational theologies!

A renewed understanding of God suffering for us, of emptying himself (*kenōsis*), for our sake, of accepting even the cross is essential if we are to escape the danger of Deism or of Islāmic *Tanzīh bilā kaif* (God's transcendence without asking how he is so transcendent!) If Christianity has anything distinctive to offer the world, it is this sense of God's nearness and openness to us, of his willingness to share our condition in order to rescue us from it.

Traditional Christology is constructive, enabling us to begin thinking creatively about the person of Christ. It may well be that 'Christology from below' should be emphasized today. Even if, however, Christological discussion begins with Jesus among the crowds in Galilee, it cannot end there if incarnational talk is to be meaningful. In such a human situation, we must be able to discern 'transcendence' in order to realize the paradox of God's disclosure in these seemingly obscure events. The context of this disclosure is important for understanding, so too is the faithful exegesis of the text. The work of hermeneutics should not, however, be ignored: God speaks to *us* through the events, through the records in all their necessary cultural conditioning. Interpretation of the saving events in our own age and our own particular context gives rise to constructive Christological thought.

Many theologies today claim to be 'people's theologies'.[23] They tend to arise out of a concern (social, economic or spiritual) for the masses. But how far do these theologies reflect the beliefs, aspirations and devotion of the masses? In Pākistān today, there is an analogous situation to that of the Church in the fourth and fifth centuries. There is a popular and passionate concern to conserve historic Christianity, and to relate it to Islām as it is experienced in Pākistān today. This concern is often expressed in devotional literature. In the country there is a mass of devotional theology in the form of poetry, allegory and hymns (the most obvious achievement of the Pākistāni Church is in the area of hymnology![24]). If we really are concerned to promote 'a people's theology', we must take these expressions of popular devotion very seriously.[25]

A study of traditional Christology then recalls us to a theology of the Incarnation, aids us in our task of theological reconstruction and reminds us of the importance of devotion in Christological thought.

CHAPTER 4

The Place of Holy Scripture in Muslim-Christian Encounter*

The Acknowledgement of Jewish-Christian Scriptures in the *Qur'ān*

As has been seen, the *Qur'ān* repeatedly claims continuity with Jewish-Christian tradition and is seen by Muslims as the last Scripture in a long line of Scriptures given to the Prophets:

> 'We believe in *Allāh* and that which was sent down on Abraham, Ishmael, Isaac, Jacob and the Tribes (of Israel) and that which was given to Moses and to Jesus and that which was given to all the Prophets from their Lord. We do not discriminate between any of them and to him (i.e. to *Allāh*) we have surrendered' (2:136).[1]

Other Scriptures are quite often mentioned, in particular the *Tawrāt* (*Torah*), the *Zabūr* (Psalms) and the *Injīl* (Gospel). Jews and Christians are challenged to live by the revealed will of God, as found in their books. The following verse is a good example:-

> 'Let the people of the Gospel judge according to that which *Allāh* has revealed therein and whoever judges not by that which *Allāh* has revealed is of the rebellious' (5:60).

A few verses earlier (v. 47) the Jews too are exhorted to live by the light of the *Torah*.

---

*Written for the Bible Society.

Muslim Apologetic regarding the Judaeo-Christian Scriptures

During the Prophet of Islām's lifetime, however, it became clear that the Scriptures of the Jews and the Christians differed markedly from the revelation which *Muḥammad* himself claimed to have received. This difficulty is countered in different ways; it is said, for example, that the *Qur'ān* fulfils the other, more partial revelations and, in certain cases, even abrogates parts of the older Scriptures. The *Qur'ānic* warrant for the doctrine of Abrogation is often found in the following passage: 'Whatever revelation we abrogate or cause to be forgotten, we bring a better one or a similar one in its place' (2:106). The verse is used to evaluate the value of other revelations *vis à vis* the *Qur'ān,* but also to determine the relation of certain later passages in the *Qur'ān* to earlier ones.[2] Another way in which the doctrine of Abrogation is discussed in the *Qur'ān* is with respect to the Jewish (or Mosaic) Law. The *Qur'ānic* view is that the Mosaic Law is mutable, that Jesus relaxed some of its restrictions and that *Muḥammad* himself relaxed others (3:50, 4:160, 5:90, 91). The *Qur'ān* then is the final, definitive revelation which fulfils the other Scriptures and where the latter contradict the *Qur'ān,* they stand abrogated.

Another way in which this difficulty has been traditionally countered is the doctrine of *Taḥrīf.* This is the belief that the Jews and the Christians have 'corrupted' or 'changed' the Scriptures in some way so that they do not agree any more with the *Qur'ān.* The *Qur'ān* itself charges the Jews and the Christians with altering the Scriptures for their own purposes (2:75–79, 4:46, 5:14, 15 etc.). Muslims are not, however, agreed as to how the Scriptures have been altered. The early Muslim commentators (e.g. *Al-Ṭabarī* and *Ar–Rāzī*) comment that the alteration is *taḥrīf bi'al ma'nī,* a corruption of the meaning of the text without tampering with the text itself. Gradually, the dominant view changed to *taḥrīf bi'al-lafẓ,* corruption of the text itself. The Spanish theologian *Ibn Ḥazm* and *Al-Birūnī,* along with most Muslims, uphold this view. However, most *Qur'ānic* scholars claim that the *Qur'ān* does not assert general corruption of the Judaeo-Christian Scriptures, but rather that texts have been misused and certain passages concealed.[3] Muslims sometimes produce an alleged book as the original Scripture which the People of the Book are supposed to have corrupted. The most well-known example of this is the so-called *Gospel of Barnabas*. This 'Gospel' which is allegedly written by St. Barnabas, a companion of Paul, has a reductionist view of the person of Christ, an exalted view of *Muḥammad* and generally attempts to find prophecies about *Muḥammad* and Islām in the teaching of Jesus.

A Christian Response to Muslim Polemic against the Bible

The doctrine of Abrogation is beset with difficulties, and it is for this reason that many Muslims reject it. Is it consistent with the *Qur'ānic* doctrine of the steadfastness and unchangeability of divine revelation? The *Qur'ān* declares quite unambiguously: 'But you will never find any change in *Allāh's* behaviour, nor will you find any alteration in it' (35:43). Furthermore, if it is held that the revelation to the Jews and the Christians was time-, people- and place-specific, why should the *Qur'ān* not also be regarded in the same way?[4] Then again, how can the *Qur'ān* be regarded as 'fulfilling' the Judaeo-Christian Scriptures? Is there more detail in it regarding the events recorded in the Bible, or a better chronology? Is the *Sharīʿah* given in the *Qur'ān* (as distinct from that later developed by the law schools) more detailed than the Mosaic law given in the *Torah*? As far as the *Qur'ān*'s relation to the New Testament is concerned, is the ethical teaching of the *Qur'ān* more elevated than that of the Sermon on the Mount?

If *taḥrīf bi'al maʿnī* (a mere distortion of the words of Scripture in speech, or a wrong interpretation of the text), is asserted, this does not challenge the Scriptures themselves and Muslims can still be invited to 'search the Scriptures'. The charge that there is *taḥrīf bi'al lafẓ* (alteration of the text itself), is more serious and has to be countered differently. If there is a discrepancy between an earlier and a later book, is the presumption not that the alteration has occurred in the later book? If it is maintained that the alteration has occurred in the earlier book, is there any evidence derived from the comparative study of manuscripts to justify such a claim? All manuscript evidence strengthens the case for the integrity of the sacred texts. The continued agreement of the Jewish Bible with the Christian Old Testament, despite the historical mutual hostility of the Jews and Christians, is an argument favouring the integrity of the Old and New Testaments.[5] The discovery of certain biblical books among the Dead Sea Scrolls has shown us that we have the same Old Testament as that which existed before Jesus. The abundance of New Testament manuscripts, the diversity of their provenance and language, their great antiquity compared to other manuscripts of ancient literature, are all powerful arguments for the integrity of the New Testament.

The attitude of Christian scholars towards the variety of manuscripts available is in striking contrast to the Muslim position that there should be only one recension of the *Qur'ān* available. As is well known, only the recension of the *Qur'ān* made under the *Caliph ʿUthman* has survived. Therefore, when a modern edition or translation of the *Qur'ān* is prepared, only one line of manuscript evidence is available.[6] When a critical edition or translation of the New Testament is being prepared, scores of more or less variant manuscripts in many different ancient languages are available, and the critical text is established by sustained comparative work on these manuscripts. This takes into account their antiquity, their currency, their use by the Fathers and other Christian writers of the time, their agreement or otherwise with other established authorities, and so on.

The survival of variant manuscripts is regarded as a strength by Christian scholars in establishing a critical text of the New Testament. The variations do not appear to compromise either the historical integrity of the New Testament or its reliability as a canon of Christian doctrine in any substantive way. The existence of a large number of manuscripts in different ancient languages, with their origins in widely separated churches yet in substantial agreement with each other, is an argument in favour of the integrity of the Scriptures.[7] Modern conservative *Maulānā Abu Aʿlā Maudūdī* claims that wherever the direct speech of a Prophet or *Rasūl* is reported in the Old or New Testament, there no *taḥrīf* is possible! *Taḥrīf* is, however, possible where there is narrative or commentary contributed by the writer or editor of a particular book. This is a remarkable view, for it leaves intact, among other things, the great discourses in John and the claim to divine authority in the Synoptics.[8]

The evidence of the 'Gospels' produced by Muslims can be countered in the following way: neither the *Qur'ān* nor early Muslim tradition ever refer to any such books. The *Gospel of Barnabas* is not mentioned by Muslim apologists until after Sale had called attention to it in his translation of the *Qur'ān*. Its earliest manuscripts are in Italian and Spanish (both modern languages!) and it disagrees with the *Qur'ān* in several important respects. The *Qur'ān*, for example, reserves the title of *Al-Masīḥ* (the Messiah) for Jesus, whereas 'Barnabas' repeatedly bestows the title upon *Muḥammad*. Again, according to the *Qur'ān*, the birth of Jesus caused Mary considerable physical pain (19:23), whereas according to 'Barnabas' his birth was painless. Many elements of dominical teaching and practice are rather naively retained from the canonical Gospels without realizing the tension this causes in relation to

Islāmic teaching. Jesus' prohibition of retaliation and the story of the woman taken in adultery are both retained and no attempt is made to reconcile them with the Islāmic teaching on retaliation and adultery. The consensus of scholars is that 'Barnabas' is a late mediaeval European forgery written possibly by a renegade monk.[9]

Christian Influences on Muslim Views of Scripture

Islām has its origins in a culture created to some extent by Christianity and Judaism. De Hart puts it this way, 'Islām has never been independent of some sort of Christian reference.'[10]

It is inevitable that there should be mutual influences on many theological matters, including views of Scripture. We have seen already the awareness in the *Qur'ān* and in early Islām of the Judaeo-Christian Scriptures, and the defence of the integrity of Scriptures made by early Christian apologists like Timothy of Baghdād.[11] There remains, however, one remarkable case of Christian influence on Muslim views of Scripture which needs to be considered. The case is that of St. John of Damascus, and the origin of the doctrine of the Uncreated *Qur'ān.* In his disputation against the Muslims, John has the Muslim admit from the *Qur'ān* that Jesus is the Word of God. The Muslim must then, according to John, admit that Jesus is the Uncreated Word, for we cannot imagine God without his Word at first and then creating it for himself. The orthodox Muslim response to this is that although God was never without his Word, this eternal Word is not Jesus but the *Qur'ān*![12] However, for John the uncreated and eternal Word must be God or there would be another eternal beside God, which would negate the unity of God. It is precisely this which Christians claim for the *Logos* and which Muslims have never claimed for the *Qur'ān*.[13] On the other hand, John distinguishes between the eternal *Logos* and the *rhēmata* of Scripture, which are the created words of God. John influenced the radical *Muʿtazila* school of theology in Islām, and it is possible that their rejection of the doctrine of the Uncreated *Qur'ān* was influenced by John's views.[14] Those Muslims who accepted Jesus Christ as a manifestation of the eternal *Logos* were from among the *Muʿtazila*, who did not have the option of taking the *Qur'ān* as the eternal Word of God.[15]

Some Muslim scholars now try to study the *Qur'ān* by using techniques developed for the study of the Christian Scriptures.[16] This has not proved acceptable to the Muslim masses and, in many places, has been abandoned. It remains true, nevertheless, that the reverent historical and textual criticism of the *Qur'ān* by Muslims themselves is vital for creative *Ijtihād* (radical hermeneutic) within the Muslim *Ummāt* (or community of faith).

Muslim Influences on Christian Views of Scripture

Muslim beliefs regarding Scripture have, perhaps inevitably, influenced Christian communities in Muslim lands. Muslims tend to think of revelation as ahistorical, mechanical and impersonal.[17] In time, these pre-suppositions affect the thinking of Christians living in Muslim countries. Scripture begins to be regarded as an oracular, 'direct' revelation of God which bypasses ordinary human means and situations. Even translations, however defective and inadequate, begin to be invested with authority which should only be accorded to the original documents. This occurs particularly where only a very small section of the Christian leadership has knowledge of and access to the original documents.

There are other attitudes to Scripture within Christian communities which have obviously come about as a result of Muslim influence. Among these would be attitudes of reverence to copies of Scripture and serious attention to the public reading of Scripture. Such attitudes are, however, also characteristic of many Eastern Christian communities.

The Authority and Inspiration of Scripture in a Muslim Context

In developing a Christian view of the authority of Scripture, full account needs to be taken of the historical, literary and human factors involved. It should be made clear that the Judaeo-Christian Scriptures have evolved over a long period of time, that their constituent parts have been written in different languages and within various cultural contexts, and that they consist of different literary types. Some books are primarily historical, some are legal and others are poetical and allegorical. Unlike the *Qur'ān*, parts of the Old Testament have survived with their integrity intact in at least three different cultural contexts: the Judaic, the Samaritan and the Christian.[18] A Christian view of the authority of Scripture would stress that God's revelation is given in and through a particular writer or editor, within a particular historical context and a particular literary medium. God does not bypass the literary or other abilities of a writer or editor, and he does not bypass history.

He uses both the strengths and the weaknesses of a particular writer or of a particular cultural context to bring his message to humankind (2 Cor. 4:7).

It is to be stressed that Scripture is a reliable and faithful record of God's saving acts in history—not of all his saving acts, but those which are interpretive of the rest of his activity in creation. This reliability is due to the work of the Holy Spirit, and may be demonstrated. Apart from the textual evidence, there is the evidence of archaeology. The discipline of archaeology owes a great deal to the scholarly study of the Bible. There is now a great deal of archaeological evidence for the authenticity of the biblical narrative. Archaeology has confirmed the antiquity of the biblical narrative, its geographical and historical accuracy, its correct use of names—in short, its complete familiarity with the cultural context in which it claims to have originated.[19]

Just as the Bible interprets the rest of history for us, so the record of the ministry of Jesus 'makes sense' of the Bible for us. It is in his teaching, his miracles, his sacrifice and its vindication that the rest of the Scriptures are fulfilled. Jesus' reverent but critical use of the Old Testament has lessons for us in the use of the Bible. Jesus understood his own ministry in terms of motifs which occur in the Old Testament, including the Servant Songs in Isaiah and the Son of Man imagery in Daniel. Jesus also regarded certain aspects of the Old Testament revelation as a record of God's will for his people at a given time in a given situation (Mk. 10:1–12, Mt. 5:21–48 etc.). His own relation to the Old Testament and to Jewish tradition was one of dynamic re-interpretation.[20]

In a Muslim context, we have to affirm the high authority of Scripture without enslaving ourselves to a non-Christian view of revelation. We need to emphasize, moreover, in our context the authority of the text as originally given. This implies, of course, a higher profile for the Scriptures in the original languages. The mere availability of these or an interlinear translation is a powerful apologetic in our context.

The Use of Scripture in a Muslim Context

A DISCRIMINATE DISTRIBUTION

Scripture distribution has a long tradition in the Muslim world. Many have come to know and to serve the Lord as a result of receiving part of Scripture. However, is is important always to be sensitive to the mood of the receiving community. In a situation, for example, where the *Sharīʿah* is being enforced, part of the Sermon on the Mount would be well received. Where there is obvious social and economic injustice, parts of the Prophets or the Epistle of James would be relevant. Where there is mystical inclination, the Gospel according to St. John would be particularly appropriate.

B SCRIPTURE SESSIONS

These can be very helpful in the form of an open class such as those conducted by certain *Ṣūfīs.* First, a period is given to teaching and then those attending are free to ask questions about the particular text under discussion or more general questions about the integrity and reliability of Scriptures.

C RELEVANT RESEARCH

This would include research on themes or characters common to the *Qur'ān* and the Bible. An excellent example is Abraham Geiger's work *Judaism and Islām*[21] where many common biblical and *Qur'ānic* words, themes and characters are discussed showing the Prophet of Islām's relation to the Bible. Another, very different, work is Geoffrey Parrinder's, *Jesus in the Qur'ān,* where the depth of the *Qur'ānic* appreciation of Jesus and its relation to canonical and apocryphal literature is discussed. The great advantage of the biblical scholar is that he can give a detailed background to events and persons only alluded to in the *Qur'ān.*

D SOCIAL SIGNIFICANCE

Christians world-wide are rediscovering the relevance of the Scriptures to the pressing social and economic issues of the day. In the contemporary Islāmic context too there is great need to emphasize the biblical teachings on love, freedom, justice, reconciliation and peace. There is further discussion of this matter in the following chapters.

> 'You search the Scriptures, because you think that in them you have eternal life; and it is they that bear witness to me' (John 5:39).[22]

CHAPTER 5

Iqbāl's Attitude Towards Other Religions, Especially Towards Christianity

ʿAllama Sir Muḥammad Iqbāl, a noted Indian nationalist who first demanded a separate homeland for Indian Muslims, is often regarded as one of the most able modern exponents of orthodox Islām, yet he had an extremely open attitude towards other religions. The true criterion of faith for *Iqbāl* is love, and not adherence to a formal system of belief.[1] *Iqbāl* believed Islām to be the final revelation of God and therefore the crown of other religious systems.[2] Nevertheless, he was willing to see that even outside Islām true love of God may be found and within Islām there may be those who have no real love for God. According to *Iqbāl,* God is not contained by any religious system but manifests himself to those who desire him ardently:

> 'You are not contained in the sanctuary, nor are you limited to the idol-temple. But how longingly you come towards those who desire you fervently!'[3]

Although God is not limited to any religious system, he may be experienced within a particular religious system. Indeed, the lover of God sees God in both infidelity and Islām:

> 'The Lover (of God) makes no difference between the *Kaʿaba* and the idol-temple, this is the Beloved's epiphany and that is His retirement into seclusion!'[4]

This represents venerable *Ṣūfī* tradition, which regarded the existence of other religions as within the providence of God and as part of his purpose. Love for God, according to the *Ṣūfīs*, is latent in all men and is, to some extent, expressed in all religious traditions.[5] God, moreover, is sovereign and can choose to reveal himself through the apparatus of heathendom. The religious system of Islām itself has value only insofar as it is a vehicle for divine revelation. If it became an end in itself, it would become worthless.

In the *Jāvīd-Nāma*, *Iqbāl* includes the Buddha and Zoroaster among the Prophets.[6] Although the *Qur'ān* restricts the title *Ahl Al-Kitāb* to the Jews and the Christians, in later Islām this was extended to include the Zoroastrians who formed an important segment of the community in the Islāmic Empire. Modern Muslims like *Sayyid Ḥussein Naṣr* have gone so far as to extend the title to all Monotheists.[7] *Iqbāl* favoured this sentiment which emphasized a worshipper's sincerity, rather than the formal religious tradition to which he may belong:

> 'An infidel with a wakeful heart before an idol,
> is better than a religious Muslim asleep in the sanctuary.'[8]

Iqbāl and Christianity

Iqbāl could not fail to be aware of Christianity. There are many references to Jesus Christ, Christians, the Church and Christianity in his works.[9] Sometimes, *Iqbāl's* use of Christian terminology is casual and without much theological significance. Such, for example, is the reference to the Trinity in the following verse:

> 'The sons (i.e. followers) of the Trinity have taken away the inheritance of Abraham. The dust of *Ḥejāz* (the cradle of Islām) has become the cornerstone of the Church!'[10]

Here, *Iqbāl* is not so much concerned with the doctrine of the Trinity as with the increase of the Christian Church in Muslim lands. Again, there is a reference to the cross: 'In the Church, they have hung the Son of Mary on a cross!'[11] Here, too, *Iqbāl* is not referring to the historicity of the crucifixion or to its doctrinal implications. He is simply deploring the use of the crucifix as a Christian symbol. The representation of a dying man is hardly an adequate symbol for a faith which offers eternal life. There are, however, parts of *Iqbāl's* work where specific Christian doctrines are mentioned and discussed quite seriously:

1. THE INCARNATION: *Iqbāl's* discussion of the Incarnation may be divided into three areas:

(a) *Iqbāl* recognizes the felt need in man for an incarnate God:

> 'O long-awaited Reality when shall I see you clothed in Phenomenality. For many thousand restless adorations wait expectantly on my suppliant brow!'[12]

And again:

> 'The eye cannot contain him', said wisdom,
> (yet) the glance of desire is in hope and fear;
> The story of Sinai does not grow old,
> The desire of Moses is in every heart!'[13]

The allusion is to the occasion recorded in the *Qur'ān* when Moses asked to see God and was told that he could not see God directly. The *Qur'ān* is ambivalent here, for in another chapter Moses does see God in the burning bush.[14] In any case, Moses' desire is regarded as typical of all humanity.

(b) *Iqbāl* seems to acknowledge the Incarnation of our Lord Jesus Christ:

> 'The Son of Mary, Lamp of the Universe,
> Incarnate and Infinite Light!'[15]

A few lines later, he has a Jewish youth tell an Eastern woman:

> 'What we have done to his humanity,
> his own community has done to his divinity!'

Just as the Jews of Jesus' day crucified the body of Christ, so the Church has crucified his divinity by failing to understand its true nature and by failing to bear true witness to it. This is a most remarkable use of the word *Lāhūt* which means Godhead, divine nature in its fullest sense.[16]

(c) *Iqbāl* is fully aware that the need for an embodied God may lead to idolatry, ascribing divinity to a person or object other than God:

> 'The desire for the presence of God is the reason for idolatry, Love deceives the soul of the hopeful'[17]

Among the *Ṣūfīs,* it became quite usual to regard one's spiritual mentor (*pīr* or *murshid*) as the abode of divinity. An example of this is *Rūmī's, Dīwān-i-Shams-i-Tabriz,* written in honour of his master. Also, *Muḥammad,* the Prophet of Islām, despite his own disclaimers and the whole weight of Muslim tradition, was increasingly referred to in incarnational terms. There were many reasons for this, not least the influence of Christian theology.[18] Although *Iqbāl* is sharply critical of the first tendency, he is much more sympathetic to the second and there are many instances in his work where a *Logos*-terminology, similar to that employed in

Christian theology and devotion, has been transferred to the Prophet *Muḥammad*:

> 'His glory created ardent desire among the angels,
> while Adam was yet unformed.'[19]

The doctrine of *Muḥammad's* pre-existence gradually developed into a doctrine of *Muḥammad* as a created *Logos* not unlike the Arian Christ. These lines from the *Jāvīd-Nāma* are even more extravagant:

> *'Except God' is the sword and its edge is 'His Servant' (i.e. Muḥammad).*
> If you want it clearer, say He (i.e. God) is 'His Servant!'[20]

2. THE CRUCIFIXION: Apart from the causal reference to the cross quoted above, there are a few other references to the cross:

> '. . . That Pilate, that Cross, that afflicted countenance . . .'

This reference, which seems to remind one both of the Apostles' Creed and Isaiah Chapter 53, is to be found in the dialogue between the Jewish youth and the European lady.[21] More significant is *Ahriman's* conversation with Zoroaster:

> 'There are poisons in His (i.e. God's) rose wine,
> the saw, the worm and the Cross are His gifts'[22]

Although the crucifixion is mentioned several times by *Iqbāl*, there is no denial (as in orthodox Islām) that it actually took place. Indeed, the implication throughout is that it occurred. *Iqbāl* holds to the *Qur'ānic* tradition that the Prophets suffered and that this suffering was a trial sent by God.[23] He ignores the ambivalence found in orthodox Islām regarding the death of Jesus and includes him among the suffering Prophets, explicitly mentioning the crucifixion. This attitude of *Iqbāl's* is consonant with *Ṣūfī* tradition, which tends to regard the cross of Jesus as the supreme example of self-denial. In the words of the poet *Naẓīrī*:

> 'He who is not slain is not of our Tribe.'[24]

According to *Ghālib*:

> 'This mystery in our hearts is not a mere sermon,
> It may only be proclaimed from the cross, not from the pulpit!'

In *Ṣūfī* tradition, a famous martyr *Ḥallāj* (d. 922 AD) is also regarded as an example of one who sacrifices self for the love of God; but Jesus is the more important figure as he is both a Prophet (*Nabī*) and a messenger (*Rasūl*) of God. Jesus, moreover, dies not simply to save himself but in the course of saving others from the consequences of their sin. In this connection, Bishop Kenneth Cragg points out that *Ḥallāj* died because he would not disclose his esoteric wisdom, whereas Jesus was crucified for preaching a kingdom of grace that could not be concealed.[25]

3. THE RESURRECTION: *Iqbāl* discusses the Resurrection of Jesus Christ within the context of the common Muslim-Christian belief in the general resurrection of the dead. The *Qur'ānic* doctrine of the Resurrection is based on the view that resurrection is a universal natural phenomenon and that, therefore, the resurrection of human beings is only to be expected.[26] The *Qur'ān* appeals repeatedly to the reappearance of vegetation after the rains as indicative of God's power to bring life to what may be regarded as dead.[27] The *Qur'ānic* doctrine of the Resurrection is, therefore, according to *Iqbāl*, very different from the Christian doctrine which bases its hope for the Resurrection of human beings on the Resurrection of an historic Person i.e. Jesus Christ.[28]

4 THE TRINITY: Apart from casual references to the Trinity such as the one mentioned above, there is an interesting argument about God's personality in *Iqbāl* which challenges the Christian doctrine of the Eternal Generation of the Son. The argument is based on Bergson's view that reproduction compromises uniqueness of personality. The Perfect Individual would not need to reproduce and, indeed, could not reproduce without compromising His perfection. *Iqbāl* refers here to certain passages in the *Qur'ān* which assert the impossibility of God begetting or generating offspring.[29]

It is disputable, however, whether reproduction compromises individuality. The reproduced individuality (at least in the higher forms of life) is not identical with the parent, although it is similar to the parent. *Iqbāl* himself admits in a well-known passage that the finite egos proceed from the Ultimate Ego, i.e. from God.[30] Would this not compromise God's perfect individuality if Bergson's view were to be accepted?

As a criticism of Christ's sonship, the argument does not apply: Christ was not conceived at a particular moment in time. He is the eternal Son of the Father and so belongs to the individuality of God. In other words, God exists eternally as Father, Son and Holy Spirit. Early Christian apologists in an Islāmic environment used illustrations like the Sun, with its light and heat, to explain the Christian doctrine of the Trinity. There is no light and heat without the Sun; but equally the Sun would not be the Sun without its light and heat. The Sun may be termed contemporaneous with its light and heat. In the same way, the persons of the Blessed Trinity are co-eternal. Another illustration used to explain the relation of the eternal Son to the Father was that of fountain and fountain-head or river and river-head: there is no fountain without a fountain-head;

but on the other hand, it is meaningless to talk of a fountain-head which has no fountain.[31] The relation of the eternal *Logos* to God the Father is not like that of the kitten to the cat but more like that of consequent to Ground (in logic) or of thought to the mind. The antecedence of the Father is logical not temporal.

Iqbāl also discusses the doctrines of Creation, Providence and Predestination. He touches on ideas on human freedom, on the nature of evil and on the worth of the individual. Islām claims to stand within the Judaeo-Christian tradition, and its theology is influenced not only by biblical thought but by later Christian theology as well.[32] *Iqbāl* re-interprets classical Islāmic doctrine in the light of the nineteenth-century philosophy of spiritual pluralism. His engagement with Christianity takes place, therefore, at two levels:

(a) The mediation of Christian influence through classical theology itself. *Iqbāl's* treatment, for instance, of the question of human freedom seems to have been influenced by the *Muʿtazila*, who in turn were influenced by the Christian theology of their day.[33] Again, we have already encountered *Iqbāl's* use of *Logos*-terminology for the Prophet. Now *Iqbāl* himself, in an early work, traces the introduction and development of this motif into Islām and acknowledges Christian influence in this area.[34]

(b) Many of the concerns of spiritual pluralism were derived from the Christian theology of the day, and these are reflected in *Iqbāl's* work. Such would be the development of a proper doctrine of creation, of divine and human freedom, of theodicy and of immortality.

Despite his conservatism, *Iqbāl* has a very open attitude towards the adherents of other religions. In particular, he had a special relationship with, and appreciation of, Christianity. This appreciation, from our point of view, was defective in some respects but profound in others.

As *Iqbāl* is the official ideologue of Islām (at least in Pākistān), his attitude towards Christianity is of the highest interest to those engaged in Muslim-Christian dialogue. There are other aspects of *Iqbāl's* work which also merit a place in Muslim-Christian encounter, although they may not be as directly related to his attitude to Christianity as the ones mentioned above. For example, *Iqbāl's* radical attitude to Islāmic Law, his emphasis on religious experience, especially prayer, and his Process Theology[35] might all be considered in this area. It is to be hoped that further study of *Iqbāl's* relation to Christianity will be carried out and that this will contribute to increased Muslim-Christian understanding and dialogue.

Part II
Missiology in Context

INTRODUCTION

It has to be understood that mission is in the first place *missio dei*, God's mission, and it is only by God's grace that the Church, which is after all a company of sinners, albeit repentant sinners, is called to participate in this mission.

God's purposes are for *all* human beings and for the *whole* person. It is, therefore, not easy to define the mission of the Church as the Church seeks to be faithful to the will of God. Provisionally, we may say that the Church should affirm, witness to and work for all that makes human beings truly human and which restores their fellowship with God. The mission of the Church then is not only the verbal proclamation of the Gospel (though this is always necessary) but also the *praxis* or living out of the Gospel in such a way that a genuine transformation is brought about in individuals, families and societies. It is also recognized that the Church will have to use its prophetic ministry of forth-telling and fore-telling on a whole range of issues which affect human well-being. This is part of bearing faithful witness to God's will for humankind and for the world.

Although the Church is called to engage in mission in such a way that human lives are changed at all levels: spiritual, physical and social; the truth remains that ultimate transformation can never be brought about on the horizontal plane alone. The Church must seek to witness to the 'transcendent horizon of the Kingdom of God'.[1] The final and ultimate act of reconciliation and transformation is God's, even as the initiative is from him. The Church herself and her work, witness and worship are proleptic 'signs' of the Kingdom. The Kingdom is present in the Church as promise and expectation. 'Signs' of the Kingdom may, however, be discerned wherever there is recognition of truth, struggle for justice or pursuit of peace.

The Church must, as part of her mission, continually reaffirm the fallenness of the world and God's judgement upon it. Even in this fallen world, however, God has not left himself without witness. The witness is found not only in creation and conscience (Acts 14:17; Romans ch. 1 and 2), but in literature and religious tradition (Acts 17:22–31). It is found, indeed, wherever men distinguish truth from falsehood. The early Fathers (such as Justin and Clement), held that whatever was true and good in human endeavour came about as a result of the illumination of the eternal *Logos* (John 1:4).[2] Such knowledge of the divine, however, is not in itself saving knowledge. Salvation is the result of our response to God's saving initiative. Necessary elements in such a response would be repentance and seeking for truth. A recognition of God's judgement upon human sin may, in itself, be the beginning of such a response. This response may occur without an explicit recognition of the historical figure of Jesus of Nazareth. It is part of the Church's mission to bring those who have such an implicit saving knowledge of God to explicit faith in Christ, which alone brings the assurance and the comfort promised in the New Testament. Coming to explicit faith in Christ is also necessary for incorporation into the community of believers, the Church. This, in turn, is necessary for nurture in Gospel values and for instruction in mission and witness. It is also to be reiterated that however salvation is experienced, it is only possible because of God's reconciling work and presence in Christ. Repentant sinners find forgiveness because of Christ's Atonement: those who seek for truth seek because their minds have first been illuminated by the eternal *Logos*.[3]

Evangelization seeks the transformation of men, women and communities. Indeed, it must also result in a continuing transformation of the Church, the agent of evangelization, itself. The Church, in seeking to share the blessings of the Gospel with others, is itself blessed.

CHAPTER 6

The Gospel's Offer of Wholeness

'To consider the World in its length and breadth, its various history, the many races of man, their starts, their fortunes, their mutual alienation, their conflicts, their aimless courses, their random achievements and acquirements, the impotent conclusion of long standing facts, the tokens so faint and broken of a superintending design, the blind evolution of what turn out to be great powers or truths, the progress of things, as if from unreasoning elements, not towards final causes, the greatness and littleness of man, his far-reaching aims, his short duration, the curtain hung over his futurity, the disappointments of life, the defeat of good, the success of evil, physical pain, mental anguish, the prevalence and intensity of sin, the pervading idolatries, the corruptions, the dreary, hopeless irreligion, that condition of the whole race so fearfully yet exactly described in the Apostle's words, "having no hope and without God in the world,"—all this is a vision to dizzy and appall.'[1]

In these moving words, Cardinal Newman describes the state of fallen human beings and the fallen world in which they live. It is a deeply Christian and biblical analysis. There are others, however, who for 'scientific', philosophical or religious reasons analyse the human state quite differently. For example, the Manichaeans both ancient and modern, locate the 'fallenness of the world' in the essentially evil character of matter. People are seen as imprisoned in evil matter, and salvation is their liberation from it. This is achieved through *gnosis* (special knowledge) of one's essential identity with some higher, non-material reality. Others believe that the origin of moral evil is in some kind of physico-chemical malfunctioning, for example, in bad genes. The solution then lies with the 'science' of eugenics. According to this view, all those unfit for producing offspring should be prevented from doing so and all those thought suitable for producing ideal children should be encouraged. In this way, an ideal kind of human being would emerge.

The idea that people are made evil through the effect of their social environment is another alternative to the Christian view. Badness is 'learnt' and does not reflect one's original state. This original state is regarded as innocent and society is blamed for the acquisition of sin. That this view is widely held is demonstrated by adherents as diverse as Jean Jacques Rousseau (18th century forerunner of humanistic liberalism) and many proponents of Islām.[2] Much modern secular thought sees human behaviour as the result both of physico-chemical inheritance *and* social environment.

In sharp contrast, the Bible, while admitting the effect of human genetic inheritance and human social environment on human behaviour, sees the will as the source of the human condition. Fr. Albert Gelin in his book *The Concept of Man in the Bible,* points out that Adam's sin is a proud claim to moral autonomy. It is a claim that human beings can decide on their own what is good and what is evil without reference to divine norms. This is a form of *hubris* (arrogance).[3] The Bible regards all humanity as somehow implicated in the sin of Adam.[4] In the Bible, the human race is 'solidary', individuals cannot be treated separately. The whole of human society is tainted with sin and no individual in it has escaped this taint. The much maligned doctrine of Original Sin may be summed up as the participation of each human being in the sinful state of the human race. It also underlines people's corruptibility, the enfeeblement of the will and the consequent inclination towards evil. The story of Adam's sin typifies the wilful arrogance of the human race against God, and in this rebellion all participate.

People do not 'acquire' evil; they are born into it and it is part of their natural condition.[5] Although, according to the Bible, the origin of the fall is in the will, the consequences of it are not restricted to the will alone, but rather affect the whole of life. This insight was recovered for the Church at the Reformation. In the heyday of Scholasticism it had sometimes been held that reason had not been affected by the Fall (how else could Aristotle's high authority be maintained?) and that Natural Theology was, therefore, possible. This view led to increased confidence in intellectual ability and may have played some part in the emergence of the Renaissance. It also led to a misplaced confidence in human ability to apprehend spiritual truth without divine revelation. In due course 'religion within the limits of reason alone' became fashionable,[6] although for the schoolmen, reason could only take one so far in the apprehension of the divine, and revelation was needed to perfect faith.

The Reformation attempted to restate the biblical view that one's whole being is affected by the Fall (and, by implication, it is the whole being that needs redemption). This is the doctrine of 'Total Depravity' mentioned, for example, in the Westminster Confession. The doctrine does not teach that people cannot do good at all or that one's faculties are wholly evil. It does teach that all of humankind's faculties, thoughts and actions are affected by the human state of sinfulness. Reason, relationships and religion are all affected by the Fall. Paul, in the first chapter of the Epistle to the Romans, allows some recognition of God by human beings, even in their fallen state, but this recognition is seen as distorted and vitiated by their disobedience.

In looking at the history of religion, the Christian must allow that even where there is some recognition of the truth in many religious traditions, that truth is distorted by the continuing human rebellion against God. For the Christian, God's unique self-disclosure in the person and work of Jesus Christ is the necessary criterion by which all human religious experience is to be judged. Jesus Christ may be seen as the fulfilment of some of the aspirations expressed in religious traditions, but he must also be seen as the Judge of these traditions. The Judaeo-Christian tradition itself, as the expression of a human response to God's revelation, must come under Christ's judgement.

The origin of sin is located in Man's will, but it affects the whole of his person and the whole of his social context. The biblical point of view is that it affects his natural environment as well. It is possible to read the biblical evidence as saying that the destruction of the natural environment, the 'curse' on it, is causally related to Man's sinful state. In other words, the destruction of the natural environment is part of human sin. Just as human beings, by their sin, have upset their spiritual and social balance, so have they upset the balance of their natural environment.[7]

Other religious traditions are also aware that a primaeval 'wholeness' has been disturbed which has affected our social relationships and also our relationships with our environment. Many (if not all) religious systems have seen the need for a return to 'wholeness'. This need is often expressed in the so-called 'Myth of the Eternal Return'. In Hindūism, for example, a primaeval, universal man (*Purusha*) offers himself as an eternal sacrifice. It is this sacrifice which causes both the diversity of creation and provides the universe with unity. Individual acts of sacrifice, made to seek a return to original 'wholeness', are identical with the eternal sacrifice which holds the cosmos together.[8]

This 'Nostalgia for Paradise' is also seen in Neo-Platonism (that great movement which was contemporary with, and a rival to, Early Christianity). Plotinus taught that the soul travels homeward by a series of ascending stations which correspond to those of its previous descent. It is finally pictured as united to the One which is its source. This Neo-Platonic doctrine of *Epistrophē* (return) is supposed to have influenced both Christian and Muslim mysticism. *Ṣūfīs,* too, teach that the soul travels back to God through an ascending series of stages or *maqāmāt* which mark human effort towards reaching the Divine Beloved. Although the *Ṣūfī* doctrine of the Return may have been influenced by Neo-Platonism, the germs of it are already in the *Qur'ān* itself.[9] In the Jewish context too, sacrifice was an act which attempted a restoration of some kind of relationship with God and of solidarity with the pilgrim community. In the Hellenistic world, to which much of the New Testament is addressed, there were many 'life-renewal' cults which emphasized the need for human beings to return to the source of their being if they are to gain immortality.

Alienation and the desire to return to wholeness is a major theme in modern discussion. According to Marx, the institution of private property and the system of capitalistic production are such that human beings cannot fail to be alienated from the product of their labour, from their social environment and from nature itself. Furthermore, the demands of capitalist society increase specialization and this is said to increase their alienation from the whole human context. Communist society is the free society where slavery to specialization (in Marx's terms 'subject idiocy') is overcome, and the worker is liberated to be authentically human. Communism claims to overcome human alienation by restoring to human beings a meaningful and free relationship to their products and to their social environment. Just as it claims to end their human exploitation by other human beings, so also it claims to regulate human exploitation of nature. It is possible to see here a reflection of some of the prophetic desire for justice and liberty, and it is indeed true that Marx remained in a dialectical relationship with the biblical tradition and did not escape its categories of thought![10] Actual Communist societies, however, have been obsessed with the structure of society and have given very little attention to the individual, with the result that instead of producing the Ideal human being, they have produced bureaucracies and new hierarchies of functionaries and specialists.[11]

The development of psychoanalysis also led to an awareness of an additional aspect of alienation: that of self-alienation or neurosis. Neurosis may be described as an inner cleavage—the state of being at war with oneself. As with Marx, the psychoanalysts were on the whole better at diagnosis than at therapy. Many psychoanalysts after Freud, however, began to see the value of religion in the restoration of wholeness to persons.

Discussion in modern times of Man's alienation is not limited to philosophy or the social sciences. Alienation is a major theme in both art and literature.[12] We find here both a radical criticism of modern industrial society and various recipes for a cure. These range from rampant millenarianism to bloody revolution, and include such socially romantic remedies (of both the right and the left), as 'interior emigration' and 'absolute refusal'.

Despite this consciousness of alienation and the felt need for a recovery of wholeness, human beings have been shown to be incapable of the 'return' they so eagerly seek. The many legal and religious systems which have evolved highlight this failure to reach the ideal. The need for a Saviour is shown by the abundance of saviour figures in the mythologies of the world. Even religions like Islām, which deny the need for a Saviour, have invested the founder of their religion or some other charismatic figure with saviour-like qualities. In Islām, for example, the Prophet is not only credited with a personality which is incarnational but he is definitely and increasingly spoken of as a saviour. This has evolved despite the absence of any such doctrine from the *Qur'ān*, and despite the view of the earliest Muslim traditionists that *Muḥammad* was thoroughly human and liable to error.[13]

The need for a saviour figure and the theme of sacrifice are often conflated to produce myths about 'dying and rising gods'. These are often connected with fertility cults and are usually vegetation gods. The god is thought to die in the winter and to rise again in the spring. There are often solemn festivals marking these events. The god is conceived as sacrificing himself for the renewal of life on the land and in the community. Such cults abounded in the ancient world and survive today, thinly disguised, even in the context of world religions. The historicity of Jesus Christ is in sharp contrast to these mythical doctrines of Return. The New Testament puts it in this way: 'For we did not follow cleverly devised myths when we made known to you the power and coming of our Lord Jesus Christ, but we are eye witnesses of his majesty' (2 Peter 1:16). Personal testimony to the person and work of Jesus of Nazareth has been given the greatest importance in the Christian Church. It is only comparatively recently that 'historicity' has been demoted in Christian theology, and that it has become possible to talk of the 'Christ of Faith' with little reference to the Jesus of History. It must, however, be stressed that we are not interested in historicity for its own sake. That which is found in history must also point beyond it if it is to have significance for our spiritual quest. Also, it must be authentic to the ideal in human beings. In some ways orthodox Islām is equally, if not more, interested in historicity, and yet it is at least open to question whether such historicity provides the kind of authentication which our spiritual search demands.

Three important aspects of the human quest for wholeness are focused in the story of Jesus: the theme of sacrifice, the Saviour motif and the search for the Ideal human being. Jesus Christ fulfils in a particular context the ageless needs and aspirations of human beings expressed in their myth, ritual and theology.

The desire to sacrifice is almost universal in the religious traditions of humankind. But sacrifice is generally limited to one's goods and chattels. It is either animals or the first fruits of a harvest that are offered in sacrifice. In the Old Testament, there is some consciousness that more may be required—both the Psalms and the Prophets realize that the offering of one's self is the true sacrifice.[14] Again, in mystical Islām the necessity for self-sacrifice is recognized. The subjugation of the *hafṣ* or self is essential if the human self is to be united with God. We saw in Part 1, Chapter 5, how Jesus Christ is often mentioned in the writings of *Ṣūfīs* as an exemplar of such self-sacrifice.

The ideal of self-sacrifice is, indeed, supremely actualized in Christ's radical obedience unto death. This sacrifice of obedience and service began at the Incarnation and is seen throughout the course of Jesus' self-giving ministry. Calvary is the dramatic culmination of this sacrifice and cannot be understood apart from the rest of the incarnation story.[15] The hopes and desires of all kinds of sacrifices (however distorted their form and rationale), are fulfilled in the sacrifice of Christ. Throughout its history, the Church has seen the sacrifice of Christ as fulfilling the hope for wholeness expressed in the sacrifices of the Mosaic Covenant, which were seen as shadows of Christ's sacrifice. In a similar way, Christ's sacrifice can be seen as a fulfilment of the hope of reconciliation and wholeness which is expressed in the sacrifices which take place within the context of other religious traditions.

This fully conscious, free obedience unto death is a definitive return to obedience for human beings. Just as Adam's sin expresses their rebellion, so the free obedience of the new Adam is the means of restoring fellowship with God. Christ provides an example of this restored fellowship and shows us a way to achieve it.[16] In other words, just as humankind's sin is to be understood as solidary and 'recapitulated' in Adam, so also humankind's return or redemption is to be understood as solidary and recapitulated in Christ.[17] Salvation 'In Christ' is just as much solidary as condemnation 'In Adam', and God's provision of salvation is directed to all humanity, to the whole *oikoumenē*.[18]

All are invited to the marriage feast, all are capable of repentance, to all the grace of God is available. God wishes all human beings to be saved. But will all be saved? Is the Universalist answer the true one? Is God's love so irresistible and inexorable that it will, eventually, overcome all human beings? The Universalist's solution is an attractive one. God's will, he says, cannot be frustrated and if God wills that all men be saved, then they will be saved. But there is another side to this debate: is it not also God's will that human beings should remain free? Is the freedom given to them in Eden to be taken away in the heavenly Jerusalem? If human beings remain free to choose, then it is possible that they will go on rejecting God to the very end. God loves all human beings, but do not some, because of their rebelliousness experience his love as wrath?[19] It may well be that some will choose eternal separation from God and will continue to value their autonomy over and above possible fellowship with God and with the saints.[20]

Universalism if interpreted in its wider, more ancient, sense to mean that God's purposes are not to be limited to a body of the elect (whether these are thought to be the nation of Israel or some sect) but embrace all humankind, is to be endorsed as biblical and Christian.[21] Election is to be understood, in its Barthian sense, primarily as the election of Jesus Christ.[22] The election of all others is a participation in Christ's election. All those who choose to open themselves to the work of the Holy Spirit and accept God's free pardon are therefore elected.

Universalism, in its narrower sense, as set forth in the doctrine of *Apocatastasis* is quite another matter. Here it is believed that all beings of a moral nature will ultimately be saved. This, we have seen, contradicts the biblical doctrine of human Freedom to accept God's freely offered grace or to reject it. The doctrine of human Freedom is crucial and central to the Christian view of humanity and to Salvation History. God *could* have saved all men by not giving them the ability to sin. There would then have been no need for a long process of God's saving work. It is, however, part of God's purpose for Man that he should be free, and come to a free obedience of God. Universalism in its narrower sense would be a gross violation of human freedom.

It is impossible for us to opt out of solidarity with Adam and his sin because of our genetic, social and moral inheritance. However, it is possible for us to opt out of the solidarity of redemption, which is in Christ. The exercise of human freedom consists of choosing between staying in Adam's sin, or accepting the offer of rescue from it.

The saviour motif is thus rescued from its mythological roots and placed firmly within the context of history. It is, however, not the context of ordinary secular history, but the special history of God's dealings with men. There is, at the moment, a reaction (in Asia at least) to 'Salvation History' theology. For example, it is felt that insisting too much on God's acts among a particular people ignores his activity among others. In other words, it 'tribalizes' God. This is a challenge to biblical theology, which needs to take seriously elements in the Bible itself which point to God's presence and activity among people other than the nation of Israel.[23]

The purpose of 'Salvation History' theology is not, as I understand it, to claim that God has worked only in and through Israel. It is rather to treat the history of Israel as an example of God's activity in the world. Jesus Christ then is the climax of biblical Salvation History but, as we have seen, he may also be looked upon as the fulfilment of the hopes and aspirations of other religious traditions, of other 'salvation histories'. Of course, it is important to remember that Salvation History does not come to an end in Jesus of Nazareth, for it continues in the Church and, in a wider sense, in the world. We have seen already that Christ is not only Fulfiller but also Judge of religious traditions. This dual role is seen clearly in Jesus' relation to Judaism. Here we have both continuity and discontinuity. Jesus was the fulfiller of the Law, yet he adopts a sharply critical attitude to aspects of the Law. He is the coming Davidic Messiah, yet he claims to transcend the concept of the Davidic Messiah.[24] Another aspect of Christ as Judge is the way in which he re-appropriates to himself (or the Church re-appropriates for him), titles which rightly belong to him but which have been usurped by historical or mythological figures. In the fourth Gospel for example, Jesus is confessed as 'The Saviour of the World'.[25] Now this was a title which was used quite freely of certain of the Roman Emperors.[26] The early Christians, quite rightly, while reverencing the Emperor, refused to honour him with this title. The Emperor was God's representative insofar as he exercized justice and maintained peace in his Empire.[27] But he was not to be confused with the incarnate, crucified and Risen Lord, who was God's provision of salvation for the world.

The work of Christ then saves us from or incapacity to return to fellowship with God. Not only with him and in him, but also behind him we return to obedience and to wholeness. It is this wholeness which is salvation in the biblical view of things. It is not merely a 'pie in the sky when you die', it is not an escape. It is rather arrival at adulthood, at full responsibility at possessing and living in eternal life, now. This would not, of course, be possible without Christ's constant presence with us and his continuous self-giving to us. His grace is continually available to us in the reading and hearing of the Word, in prayer and in the sacraments which he has instituted.

'All the way to heaven, is heaven,
For has he not said I am the Way.'

—St. Catherine of Siena

CHAPTER 7

Mission as Freedom to Serve*

> 'A dispute also arose among them, which of them was to be regarded as the greatest. And Jesus said to them, 'The kings of the Gentiles exercise lordship over them; and those in authority over them are called benefactors. But not so with you; rather let the greatest among you become as the youngest and the leader as one who serves. For which is the greatest, one who sits at table, or who serves? Is it not the one who sits at table? But I am among you as one who serves'' ' (Luke 22:24–27).

The disciples are still in bondage to the expectations of their culture at this point. They expected their 'greatness' as disciples of Jesus to be analogous to 'greatness' as recognized by their own culture and their own time. Jesus issues a radical challenge to their bound understanding. He seeks to liberate them from slavery to their cultural mores. It is this liberation which leads them to radical service. It is interesting to note that in Mark this teaching is followed by the 'ransom' saying (Mk. 10:45). In other words, 'liberated service' is to imitate Jesus himself. The central importance of this teaching may be judged by the fact that it occurs in all four Gospels. In the Synoptics, it is more or less in this form, and in John it is in the context of the 'acted parable' of the washing of the feet. In all four, the context is the approaching passion of our Lord. In the Synoptics, it accompanies his rejection of temporal notions

---

*Based on a keynote address to the National Council of Churches, 1984.

of messiahship, especially at the time of the triumphal entry into Jerusalem.

The text is not merely about true 'Christian greatness' *vis à vis* the world, but also about greatness in the Church. The dispute arose *among* the disciples and there is at least a hint about leadership in the Church. The 'elders' or 'presbyters' are to be humble in their behaviour towards the other believers, the *episkopos* must have an aspect of *diakonos* to be a truly Christian *episkopos*. As one commentator puts it, '. . . the point is that all Church leaders must show the characteristics of those who are especially entitled "deacons" .'[1]

Let us now go to the Scriptures to see what freedom and service mean there. In the New Testament *eleutheros* (freedom) is understood as: freedom from bondage to the principalities and powers; freedom from disease; and freedom from bondage to the Law. The metaphor used here is that of *lutron*, a price paid for the ransom of a slave or prisoner of war. But while a personal understanding of deliverance is basic to the Gospel, this is parallelled by the social dimension: personal freedom has immediate social consequences. In highlighting the social dimension of freedom, 'liberation theologians' have quite rightly pointed to the proclamation of *Jubilee* by Jesus in the Nazareth Manifesto (Lk. 4:16f).[2] *Jubilee*, for the Jews, was not only a time of celebration and social renewal but of liberation. Jesus was not, however, satisfied with the Jewish *Jubilee* (with which his own ministry may have begun), but looked forward to a tremendous universal liberation or *Jubilee*, the coming of the *Malkuta Yahweh* (or Kingdom of God, the establishment of God's personal sovereignty over all).[3] In the Old Testament, freedom from oppression, both external and internal, is a characteristic feature of the Kingdom of God.

Both Ezekiel and Jeremiah speak of the deliverance of the people of God from the oppression of those originally appointed to lead them, spiritually and temporally. The exilic Prophets, of course, emphasize the deliverance from foreign oppression whereas Amos emphasizes the judgement of those who exploit the less fortunate and the promise of God's just rule being established. Therefore, for the biblical writers, the establishment of a just social order is a necessary consequence of their understanding of God's holiness. In fact, it is precisely this element in Hebraic religion which distinguished it from many other Middle Eastern religious traditions.

The New Testament uses two words for service: *diakonia* and *doulia*. For some reason, the former has been greatly emphasized in the Church's understanding of service. Perhaps use of the term in the liturgy has made it more acceptable. Deacons, of course, had fixed liturgical duties but they also filled the role of a social worker in the early Church. It is interesting to note that both male and female deacons—the same word is used for both—were known in the early Church. Liturgical duties, however, seem to have been carried out only by male deacons.[4]

Doulia has not attracted as much attention, even though it is used in the key kenotic passage in Philippians Chapter 2. Here the eternal *Logos* is spoken of as assuming the form of a *doulos* or slave. Again, in the acted parable of the washing of the feet recorded in John 13, Jesus sets aside his garments and girds himself with a *lention,* or towel used by a menial slave in the washing of his master's feet.[5] When attention is turned to Jesus as *doulos,* it is often his self-understanding as the *'Ebed Yahweh* (Servant of God) of Deutero-Isaiah which is meant. It is clear, however, from John 13 that Jesus regarded himself as the slave of those he had come to serve as well. Moreover, both John 13 and Philippians 2 regard Jesus' radical humility as a model for his disciples: 'have this mind in you, which was also in Christ Jesus . . .'

How are biblical ideas of freedom and service to be interpreted in the contemporary world? The bondage of modern human beings is expressed both in 'structural sin'[6] and in the disintegration of human personality which results from sin. The term 'structural sin' includes all social systems, customs, kinship groups, guilds, etc., which obstruct the full development of human personality and the nurturing function of society. This umbrella term includes both crude graspings for power and money as well as more sophisticated systems which aim to control every aspect of human behaviour.

A major aspect of 'structural sin' is the alienation of race from race, class from class, human being from human being and product from producer. According to Marx, in a capitalist system the worker is alienated from the fruit of his labour because the product does not belong to him. He is simply a factor in the cost of production. Marx explained this by means of a simple equation: if C is the cost of the raw material required for production, V the cost of labour and S is the surplus value of the article, then the total value of a product will be C+V+S. Now in the equation C+V+S= Value, it is the distribution (or lack of distribution) of S which is the root of exploitation in capitalist societies. Marx was not, as is commonly understood, against profit. Profits are necessary for the growth of industry. But S, in capitalist societies, is not mere profit, it is the capitalist's income even though he has had no part in production. It is S, therefore, which makes this equation an equation of suffering.[7] Even if the capitalist should get a return for entrepreneurial risk, the proportion of S to V is still grossly unjust.

In other words, in capitalist societies, the availability of capital (and, it might be said, of capital-related skills) is given excessive importance over and above the use of other skills and labour.

Actual communist societies, however, have not done away with this kind of alienation. The worker is still alienated from his product and the place of the capitalist has been taken by a faceless state bureaucracy. Marx, of course, understood quite well that the alienation of the worker from his product is related to other kinds of social alienation. Communist societies have not always been successful in overcoming these other kinds of alienation either. Marx quite rightly pointed out that the urgent need was not merely to interpret but to change.

How is the Christian and the Church to respond to 'structural sin'? First, Christians must reaffirm for themselves and for others the strongly egalitarian basis of Christian social philosophy; 'Here there cannot be Greek or Jew, circumcized and uncircumcized, barbarian, Scythian, slave, free man, but Christ is all and in all' (Col. 3:11). In addition, Christian notions of equality cannot be restricted to those within the community of faith. The parable of the good Samaritan, in agreement with the Old Testament teaching, makes it impossible for us to treat those within the Church differently from those outside (Lk. 10:29–37; cf. Matt. 25:31–46; Lev. 19:13–18, 33). The early Christians were more or less democratic even in the area of ecclesiastical policy; bishops and other Church leaders were elected by acclamation (this still survives in a small way in the ordination services of the Church),[8] slaves could be elected to positions of leadership, masters and slaves shared in the same sacrament at the Eucharist, and so on. The early Church did not confront the secular powers on the question of slavery but rather subverted the ideology of slavery. There can be no greater contrast than that between Aristotle's view of slaves as 'living tools' and St. Paul's declaration that slaves were as much heirs of the new humanity in Christ as anyone else (1 Cor. 12:13; Gal. 3:28; Col. 3:11).

Our modern notions regarding human dignity, human rights and human freedom owe a great deal to the egalitarian thinking of the early Church. In the early days, as today in many areas, Christianity was regarded as a religion of slaves and, as such, was and today can be, a genuine movement of the proletariat offering equality to all. Freedom in Christ, however, is more than mere emancipation, it is liberation to serve. The Gospel demands that we move rapidly from notions of the equality of all men to those of mutual service. It is this 'free service' which is the imitation of Christ and which liberates both the Christian and those whom he seeks to serve. 'Thy service is perfect freedom,' we pray and this includes both the experience of release which worship should bring and the freedom which serving others brings. In seeking to bring freedom to others the Christian is both a revolutionary and an ameliorist; both challenging structures which perpetuate injustice and working within them to reduce the effects of oppression and injustice.

Do we experience this kind of freedom in our Churches today? It is urgent that we should inculturate the Gospel into our context. We do not need to detach ourselves from our background in order to serve Christ, although we must lose much of our cultural baggage and thus become aware of our superstitions and prejudices. It is only when we are critically aware of our own culture that we can seek to change it and to imbue it with Gospel values. The ruling concept of *ʿizzat* (honour) in Pākistān, and other Asian and Middle Eastern lands, for example, prevents many from adopting a truly servant role *vis à vis* our own people and outsiders. Concepts such as these tend to keep class, caste and kinship stratification intact, and there is a need to be liberated from them to liberate society. This is precisely the point of the kenotic passage in Philippians Chapter 2: Christ Jesus made himself of no account, accepted dishonour for our sakes, so that we may be reconciled to God.

Are Church-run institutions agents for change in this respect? Do they encourage their members to take a more creative and liberating role in society, or are they simply reinforcing elitist attitudes and prejudices? In other words, do Gospel-values permeate our rationale for operating these institutions or are there other reasons?

The Church has often been in the fore-front of the development of education and medicine.[9] But have we been comprehensive enough? Have we paid enough attention to adult education (especially female adult education), for example? Have we treated the development of preventive medicine and community health as of top priority? We have discovered recently how both of the above are closely related; literate mothers can be given literature regarding such things as a balanced diet for their families and the treatment of diarrhoea in infants. Literate men can be given simple instructions regarding the improvement of drains in their locality (in terms of simple drawings and so on). There are groups of dedicated Christians who are prophetically engaged in such ministries, but their number is small and they do not receive enough financial and moral encouragement from the Church.

It is often said that the emphasis that Luther and the other reformers put on the right of individual Christians to read and to appropriate the Scriptures for themselves was instrumental in creating a climate in Western Europe which lead ultimately to a universal respect for human freedom at all levels. More contemporary is the example set by the Korean Christians during the first half of this century when they refused to worship at Shinto shrines during the Japanese occupation.[10] This act, and others like it, identified Christianity with the national aspirations of the Korean people and is a significant factor in the phenomenal growth and influence of the Church in Korea. The Church must bear a prophetic witness to the world opposing injustice, tyranny and deprivation of freedom wherever she finds them, if she is to continue to be a light to lighten the nations.

We have seen already that a change of mind in the individual and the community is necessary to bring about genuine transformation. This is being brought about through 'agents of change' who motivate and conscientize the people among whom they work. It is precisely this 'change of mind' which the New Testament calls *metanoia*, and which is the basis for all Christian transformation.

Human beings do not just need deliverance from oppressive structures and from economic injustice, they need deliverance from themselves, or rather, from what they have become. The psychotic disintegration of the human personality as a result of social and personal sin is an increasing and frightening phenomenon in the world today. The Church genuinely needs to be seen as a restored and whole community, incorporation into which can heal the emotional wounds caused by a fallen world. It is only as a reconciled community that the Church can offer reconciliaton to the world.

The 'vertical' aspect of reconciliation for the Christian is, quite rightly, often stressed, but we need also to recognize the necessity for the 'horizontal' aspect. We need to be reconciled to God, but that reconciliation should result in being reconciled to other men and to oneself. Ultimately, of course, it is the grace of God experienced through faith in Christ which restores in us the image of God spoilt by sin. There are, however, ways in which the Church can help; spiritual counselling has long been recognized as one of the ways in which a mature Christian can help another Christian who is facing problems. This may take the form of confession in the presence of a presbyter, or take place in a more informal atmosphere. The Church of Pākistān provides for both methods. The Anglican Prayer-Book puts it in this way:

> 'Therefore if there be any of you, who by this means (private examination) cannot quiet his own conscience herein, but requireth

> further comfort or counsel, let him come to me (i.e. the Priest) or to some other discreet and learned minister of God's Word and open his grief; that by the ministry of God's Holy Word he may receive the benefit of absolution, together with ghostly (i.e. spiritual) counsel and advice, to the quieting of his conscience, and avoiding of all scruple and doubtfulness.'[11]

The involvement of an authorized minister of the Church is necessary for such spiritual counsel to assume a 'sacramental' aspect, but spiritual counsel may be offered by other Christians in the context of the family, for example, or in a fellowship group or even in the context of Christian institutions. The development of true fellowship in congregations is another way to help the reintegration and development of personality. All of us need to feel accepted and welcome. The Church must maintain the tension between its universal appeal to all and its desire to treat each person specially. The existence of small groups for fellowship within congregations where individuals are known, cared for and prayed for is absolutely essential for the maintenance of a pastoral ministry that is truly caring and which encourages a truly deep sharing between Christians.

The experience of grace in worship and in prayer is another way in which personalities can be healed. Corporate worship should be organized in such a way that such a healing experience is made possible. The preaching ministry of the Church too should emphasize the 'wholeness' of salvation which Jesus Christ desires and provides for us. It is not just that our sins are forgiven but the whole of our personality is recreated. Our hurts are healed, our minds are transformed, our hearts are renewed. The Helper, or the *Paraclete*, enables us to assume and to maintain this new humanity in Christ.[12]

As long as the world remains fallen and humanity fractured, ultimate 'wholeness' of personality cannot be achieved. The Church must, nevertheless, be seen to be the first fruits of the coming Kingdom of God. Therefore, there should be as much social 'wholeness' within the community of faith as is possible, and this should be reflected in the lives of individual Christians. Furthermore, the Church must, however difficult it may seem, continue to offer and to mediate this wholeness to the world by Word, sign and act.

> 'The nightingale sang of servitude in the Garden as true freedom,
> The faithful claim that it is servitude of Paradise,
> My warnings[13] have however been transformed into the good news;
> that it is the service of the suffering servant which is true freedom!'

CHAPTER 8

Contextualization: The Bible and the Believer in Contemporary Muslim Society*

To open God's Word to all means to make it possible for all to understand it. The task of interpretation is a prerequisite for evangelization. It is necessary for those who are called to preach the Word to seek understanding as to how the Word was experienced and appropriated by those who first received it. Those who would be teachers of the Word should seek first to understand the culture, the language, the religious context and the economic conditions prevailing at the time a particular revelation was received. It is also incumbent on the evangelists and the catechists to understand the cultural milieu to which they address themselves. They must have some knowledge of the history, literature, art and psychology of the people to whom they seek to communicate the Gospel. They should be aware of how the human situation has been understood in that culture. Such interpretations of the human predicament may range from psychoanalysis to economic analysis (in our own context, a knowledge of Islām in the classical sense as well as of subcontinental Islām and the way in which both have affected the development of Islāmic polity is extremely important). We need also to take account of factors like caste and its influence on class structure,[1] economic exploitation as part of our feudal agrarian system and the emergence of an industrial proletariat.

---

*Written for the Bible Society.

The faithful and meaningful translation of the Scriptures into the receptor languages is vital for evangelization, and yet often taken for granted. How to transfer the meaning of the text in the source language to that in the receptor language is the fundamental problem faced by all translators. On the whole translators are aware that they are not preachers or evangelists. They cannot arrogate to themselves the task of interpretation. But how faithfully can they adhere to the form in the source-language without doing violence to the meaning in the receptor language? On the other hand, abandoning the form altogether may result in a Bible that is culture-specific, thus isolating the Christian community that uses it from the rest of the universal Church. The translator then needs to be sensitive enough to produce a translation which is meaningful to the culture which receives it, while at the same time preserving the form, the metaphors and the images of the original as far as possible.

One insight which biblical criticism has afforded us is that the Bible consists of diverse kinds of material written by different kinds of people at different levels of literary achievement. It may be useful, therefore, for translators to consider very carefully the kind of material they are translating and then to adopt the form in the receptor language most analogous to it. St. Mark's Gospel then may very possibly be translated into a popular form, but the Song of Songs would need a literary rendering. In the same way, St. John's Gospel would need at least some use of philosophical-theological terminology, whereas the Revelation of John may use the language of religious experience in a particular culture.[2]

Tradition and Metaphor

Hermeneutics is the interpretation of metaphors developed within one area of discourse to those of another area of discourse. The diverse metaphors of Scripture and of cumulative Christian tradition need to be reinterpreted for the contemporary community of faith. Secondly, the community of faith needs to interpret its metaphors to the wider community in which it finds its locus.

How are the metaphors in Scripture and tradition to be appropriated today? There are a number of ways in which 'the ice may be broken' or 'the penny dropped'. An important instance for us today is undoubtedly where our problems and experiences (both social and personal) reveal the significance of the biblical or traditional metaphor for us. Thus our experience of the poor, the disadvantaged and the marginalized highlights for us the evangelist's concern to portray Jesus among the crowds or Jesus with the outcastes or Jesus dealing with foreigners. A particular domestic situation may highlight the parable of the prodigal son for us in a new way. When our contemporary situation is seen as analogous to the situation of original disclosure, then the latter acquires a special significance for us. The task of hermeneutic is bound to take history, both sacred and contemporary, with the utmost seriousness. Nevertheless, it is equally important to understand that metaphors are necessary for the interpretation of historical processes.

When in dialogue with a non-Christian community, Christians should be willing to acknowledge that the very different metaphors of another tradition may reflect the same reality as the Christian metaphors do. On the other hand, there may be a genuine lack of metaphors regarding a certain area in the other tradition. Equally there may be a lack of metaphors in the Christian tradition in a certain area where the other tradition is rich in metaphors. One tradition, for example, may lack metaphors for God perceived as personal, while another may lack metaphors for a state so much beyond pain and suffering that it is regarded as beyond existence itself.

In our Islāmic context today, we have to recognise the tremendous efforts being made by our Muslim brethren in enforcing the *Sharīʿah* (the law of Islām) in society. The ruling metaphors here have to do with the establishment of God's just reign in the Islāmic *Ummāt* (or Community of faith). In dialogue with the Muslim, the Christian will affirm such ruling metaphors both in Islām and in his own tradition. He may, however, point out that in his tradition a zeal for enforcing God's will has often led to grave injustice rather than justice. Again from his tradition he may highlight the dangers of legalism and develop the metaphors of grace and of 'a righteousness which exceeds the righteousness of the Scribes and Pharisees' (Matt. 5:20).

Frustration with the enforcement of *Sharīʿah* and increasing awareness of the failure to observe the law (both by communities and individuals) should not lead to an impasse but to a recognition that it is God who by his grace enables us to keep his law. Dialogue in this context will highlight the perception by both Muslims and Christians that behind the Law of Moses and the *Sharīʿah* there is a 'greater law of love', without which any 'enforcement' of law is futile. An experience of 'grace' in this context may lead us to understand this greater law of love which is a negation of mere retribution, restriction and reduction and is an affirmation of reformation, rehabilitation and reconstruction. Dialogue in the

Muslim world today will sharpen the Christian's perception of elements in his tradition which emphasize both God's justice and his love, which stress the importance of interior renewal and which affirm the possibility of unconditional love for one's neighbour.

In our concern for a new world order, we have to affirm with those of other traditions our common desire for justice and peace. However, we have to bring the distinctive witness of the Gospel to our context and to relate it to our societies' search for justice and peace.

Inculturation

In the context of Islām this is a cyclical problem, i.e. how much is there in Islām which is related, directly or indirectly, to Christian sources? The influence of Christian monasticism on *Ṣūfīsm* and the influence of the later Fathers on the development of *Kalām* or formal theology in Islām is well established.[3] It is also known that many of the early mosques had been Christian churches and the influence of oriental Christianity is readily apparent in Muslim architecture. If, therefore, Christians in a Muslim context decide to build Churches that look like mosques they are only reappropriating something they have in common with Islām.[4] There are many other areas of influence.

The example of the ancient Churches in Islāmic lands is particularly valuable in this context. As we have seen, there is a great deal that Islām owes to them, but the oriental Churches adapted as well. This adaptation was both social and cultural; they learnt to live as a politically powerless minority which, nevertheless, wielded great influence culturally and commercially. In matters of social etiquette, etc., they made every effort to adjust. Sometimes, of course, they had no choice in the matter. The dress of the Coptic clergy, for example, was regulated by the state and continues to be so even today! They adopted the language of the ruler (Arabic) for day to day social intercourse, although they kept their own ecclesiastical and liturgical languages alive as well.

Eventually they adopted '*Allāh*' as their usual word for God, though there had been some early polemic against it. When the Bible came to be translated into Arabic, *Allāh* was used as the word for God. In the translation of the liturgies too, *Allāh* is often used. Many of their characteristics of worship, such as attitudes of reverence and the wealth of symbolic language in the liturgies, are, in any case, consonant with Muslim culture. So are socio-liturgical practices such as the segregation of the sexes during divine worship. The early Church rejected the practice of excluding women from the body of the synagogue but retained segregation of the sexes. The ancient Churches continue this practice to a large extent. Despite adaptations, the ancient Churches maintain a vigorous counter-culture which witnesses to Gospel values.

Contextualization in Pākistān Today

Culturally at least, the *Punjābī* Church is well integrated into the community. *Punjābī* Christians speak the same language, have the same life-style and the same problems as their Muslim *Punjābī* brethren. Some problems, however, remain, and these include the kind of 'petty apartheid' which operates against poorer Christians because some of them are sweepers. This is a Hindū hangover in Muslim Pākistān. In Islām, of course, there should be no caste consciousness, but sweeping is regarded as an unclean profession among caste Hindūs.

As far as worship is concerned, the *Punjābī* Psalms are well contextualized and non-Christians admire their language and the classical *'raags'* to which they are usually set. (It may be worth pointing out that Psalm 37 in *Punjābī* uses *'Allāh'*).[5]

The translation of the Bible into Persian *Urdū* has achieved the status of literature. Contrary to the belief in some Western missiological circles,[6] the Bible in *Urdū* has an idiom that is thoroughly Indo-Muslim and its language is much admired and used in Muslim literary circles.

The language of the liturgies is becoming increasingly contextualized. In some churches, for example, the Gospel is now sung in the way the *Qur'ān* is chanted (the cyclical nature of contextualization in an Islāmic context is illustrated here; the chanting of the *Qur'ān* is related to the singing of the lections in the Syrian Christian liturgies. Indeed the word *'Qur'ān'* itself is related to the Syriac *qeryana* which means the scripture reading!).[7]

Christians in Pākistān today face the dilemma of whether contextualization should take place with reference to folk-culture or with reference to orthodox Islām. A case in point is the development of indigenous Christian music and its use in worship. In orthodox Islām, the use of musical instruments in worship is forbidden although such instruments are widely used in *Qawwālīs* (a popular folk-devotion). In Christian worship, too, indigenous musical instruments are commonly used and, indeed, many of the forms of indigenous Christian music have been borrowed from *Qawwālīs*. Contextualization has occurred here at the level of folk-culture. The problem is being experienced in a sharper way in the South, where many tribal Hindūs are becoming Christian. The Church is busy contextualizing the worship of these new Christians according to their Hindū folk-culture. Thus a great many *bhajans* are being produced. These are songs which narrate the events of the Gospels in the way that the Hindūs used to narrate the events of the Hindū epics. Again, at weddings, instead of going around the fire as was their previous custom, Christian couples go around the cross. The problem is that ultimately these Christians will have to come to terms with Pākistāni culture which is, increasingly, Muslim culture. How far then should contextualization into the Hindū context be encouraged?

Without touching on the possibility of syncretism (which may become a problem), there are areas of difficulty as far as contextualization is concerned. There is, for example, in our context, the uncritical acceptance of the Muslim world-view. Then there is the subconscious acceptance of the Muslim theory of revelation and its application (or misapplication) to the Christian Scriptures. This has caused many problems in Pākistān, sometimes even resulting in schism. At times there is a conscious desire to imitate as, for instance, in the attempt by certain Christians to provide an alternative 'Christian' system as an equivalent to the Muslim *Sharīʿah*. Christian women will sometimes adopt *purdah* when they achieve a certain socio-economic status. On occasions, attempts are made to 'Christianize' superstitions. An example of this is the way the consecrated elements are sometimes used to prepare amulets. At the level of worship too, there seem to be undesirable influences such as the tendency to preach repetitive, exhortatory sermons at the expense of expository ones and the increasing use of loudspeakers fixed outside churches.

A historical perspective of Christian attempts at contextualization compels us to ask certain questions about the process. First, how much diversity is permissible? In other words, what minimum uniformity should there be? The early Church permitted a great deal of cultural adaptation; but Scripture, the dominical sacraments, and the unity and mutual recognition of ministries set limits to what was permissible. It is possible to imagine a Church today which has a 'dynamic equivalence' translation of the Bible, contextualized sacraments (yoghurt and *nān* in one local instance) and a radical view of ministry. The question remains, as to what continuity such a Church would have with the Church through the ages and round the world? Should there be a distinctive Christian counter-culture in a given society or should Christians integrate as much as possible? Should we be as lights, clearly seen but separate, or should we be as salt or leaven, changing society from the inside? Perhaps these two models are not mutually exclusive.[8]

The ancient Churches in Islāmic lands, at any rate, have managed both to retain and to develop their own counter-culture and to influence their society at large in the fields of education, commerce and even politics. Their situation has not allowed them to evangelize openly, but there *are* signs that these Churches are becoming aware of their obligation in this area, although there are serious obstacles in their way in carrying out the Great Commission. We need to pray that the new signs of life in these Churches will be nurtured and allowed to grow. A great deal of distinctive Christian witness in an Islāmic context depends on this happening.

CHAPTER 9

Evangelization: A Profile*

The word evangelization encompasses the whole process of communicating the Gospel: pre-evangelism, evangelism and discipling. It is, therefore, an activity directed at both Christians and non-Christians. The non-Christians are to be challenged to consider the claims of Christ, and the Christians are to be confronted with the personal and social implications of the Gospel.

Ministry to Non-Christian Enquirers

Many people are seeking an alternative life-style. Some look for meaning, others a definite system of values which could order their lives. Many of them are ready to consider the way of the Gospel.

It is often asked, 'What are enquirers like?' Although it is impossible to categorize people neatly, certain broad generalizations can be made. In terms of socio-economic stratification, most enquirers come from the lower-middle classes although there are some upper-class and poor enquirers as well. Most enquirers are between the ages of twenty and thirty, and many have been or are students. Most of them are men, though the number of women enquirers is on the increase. Many are dissatisfied with social and cultural conditions. Their dissatisfaction may be directed broadly at the way in which society is organized, or, more specifically, they may object to the treatment of women, or the extent to which

*Prepared for the Christian Conference of Asia.

political dissent is tolerated. There may also be psychological or domestic reasons for their alienation from their social setting. Social maladjustment of this kind amongst converts and enquirers is one of the most neglected areas in contemporary missiological thought.

Some enquirers are attracted to the ethical teaching of Jesus, as found for example, in the Sermon on the Mount. They regard Christianity primarily as a prescriptive lifestyle according to which they could order their lives. Others have had a specific religious experience with a 'Christic' content and wish to make further spiritual exploration. Such an experience may be one of healing or of a vision or revelation of some kind. (Some recent testimonies include: *I Dared to Call Him Father*, by Bilquis Sheikh, *The Torn Veil*, by Sister Gulsham Esther, and G. M. Naaman's *The Unexpected Enemy*).

The kind of approach adopted by the church in this profile[1] varies with the kind of enquirer. An enquirer in the first category, for instance, needs much more doctrinal grounding than an enquirer from the second category who is usually quite acquiescent in accepting Christian doctrinal formulations. The latter, however, needs quite often to be made more aware of the moral implications of the Gospel.

The church ministers to new enquirers in a variety of ways. It may receive enquirers who come to the church premises and by arranging for their instruction. The church makes available evangelistic literature in church buildings and holds special campaigns during which evangelistic literature is widely distributed. It supports the work of St. Andrew's Brotherhood, a local organization which exists to provide information, instruction and support to enquirers. The church prepares the various house-groups to be ready to accept new believers and to help them to integrate. Some members and clergy are involved in the work of an organization which is developing a centre for holistic mission in a hitherto 'unchurched' area. This centre will involve a resident evangelist, a book room, regular worship and a tuition centre for underprivileged students and some medical work. A stewardship programme based on the giving of the various house-groups enables the church to support the work of various parachurch organizations which are engaged in mission and evangelization.

Dialogue

Dialogue has been defined as 'a mood, a spirit and an attitude

. . .'[2] Those at the Cathedral church are aware that they have been placed in this particular context by divine providence and are anxious to develop relations of mutal trust, respect and good will with their non-Christian neighbours. They believe that their attitude towards their neighbours should always be one of respectful attention to what they have to say, with a desire to share the Gospel with them.[3] Dialogue, however, cannot be simply an attitude, there must be *praxis*.

Dialogue may take place in different settings and take different forms. Members of the church staff have been involved in what may be called official dialogue. This may be conducted at the international level under the aegis of the World Council of Churches, such as the Muslim-Christian Consultation at Colombo in 1982. Equally, it may be conducted at the national level such as the meetings organized by the Christian Study Centre in Rawalpindi. Such dialogue is usually conducted between two organizations, one Christian and the other Muslim. The agenda may be drawn from problems facing both communities, or from the perception of one community which sees the other as the one that creates problems for the first. Theological affinities and differences may also be tackled.

Semi-official dialogue may be conducted at a more local level between (say) a parish and a mosque or between two local groups. Members of the Cathedral have been involved, for instance, in dialogue with a team of *Aḥmadiyya* missionaries and with a militant Muslim student organization. Dialogue may also be conducted in a classroom setting between a Christian teacher and non-Christian pupils, or between a non-Christian teacher and Christian pupils.

Finally, there is the person-to-person or family-to-family dialogue which is conducted in a social setting. Such dialogue may occur between neighbours or between two friends. This kind of dialogue is often the most meaningful and the most fruitful. Members of the Cathedral, particularly members of the house-groups, are deeply involved in this kind of dialogue.

In terms of content, the parish is involved in a continuing dialogue with non-Christian groups concerning the provision of social and medical services in the *bustī* (or slum) areas. When inoculation teams go to a particular area, they often ask the local mosque to use their loudspeakers to inform the residents of the locality of the team's arrival. Both Muslim and Christian children are immunized. At another level, the parish is actively engaged in the development of dialogue with a reformist *Ṣūfī* order in Lahore. The content of the discussion, in this case, tends to be an exchange of views on religious experience, particularly on prayer and meditation. Most dialogue, however, tends to be discursive; it is an exchange of information about the teaching and history of various faiths or a presentation of apologetic material from one side to the other. Muslim friends, neighbours and sometimes even organizations, often ask Christians questions about the Sonship of Christ, the Blessed Trinity or the integrity of the Holy Scriptures. There is a great deal of Christian apologetic material available on these issues and a Christian can present a Muslim friend with relevant material.[4]

There is continuing tension between 'evangelicals' and 'ecumenicals', and within the Ecumenical Movement itself, as to whether dialogue is to be used for evangelization or whether it is an end in itself. On the one hand the Chambesy Statement is quite clear that dialogue must not become a means for evangelization.[5] On the other, preparatory material circulated by ecumenical organizations like the Christian Conference of Asia for their own consultations not only countenance the idea of dialogue as a means of evangelization, but positively encourage it.[6] The present writer was privileged to help in the drafting of a statement on dialogue a few years ago. The statement agreed that 'proselytizing' is to be rejected as sub-Christian, that the freedom and integrity of our non-Christian partners is to be respected. Nevertheless, it goes on to declare that dialogue should have an evangelistic dimension:

> 'Certainly, it is incumbent upon us to witness with the greatest sensitivity and sympathy; but witness we must, even, and perhaps especially, in the context of dialogue.'[7]

Diakonia

Deacons (those set aside for service), in the early Church did not wait for the needy to come to them, rather, they went out to find the needy and to help them.[8] Those at the Cathedral are trying to break out of a mould which has trained them to expect those in need to come to them. They are trying to make their congregations more mission-minded, and in this respect they have developed several-outreach programmes which seek to minister to the needs of the whole man. In one *bustī*, for instance, they have provided, in addition to pastoral care, a whole range of services ranging from adult literacy for women and child care, to a medical and human development programme. In another, they have regular Bible studies and worship. They have also created a 'Christian presence' in the brick-kilns and are, at the moment, examining ways of bringing meaningful change in the lives of these people who really may be called 'the submerged tenth'.[9]

The congregation are encouraged to give to and be involved in projects for the handicapped and the underprivileged. The house-groups too, through their stewardship programmes, participate in this ministry. Young people are being conscientized to offer themselves for Christian service and for evangelistic ministry.

Evangelization and Social Service

Christian service is to be offered to our fellow human beings without thought of reward. In addition, it is not to be used to 'bribe' people into the Kingdom. What then is the precise relationship between evangelization and social service? There are several 'reductionist' answers available both from the theological left and the theological right. One extreme would hold that the Church has no business in getting involved with the process of social change and should not challenge existing social structures. It should, rather, concentrate on proclaiming the good news of salvation and when men have repented and become new, then meaningful social change would automatically follow. The other extreme would, more or less, identify the social work of the Church with evangelization. For them, the humanization of society brought about through the promotion of social justice, the ending of class exploitation and peaceful coexistence, ushers in the Kingdom of God.

The present writer agrees with the Consultation on the Relationship between Evangelism and Social Responsibility (CRESR)[10] that social concern is a necessary consequence of evangelism and also that it may be a bridge to it. General Frederick Coutts of the Salvation Army has said that the evangelical and the social work of the Army were 'two activities of the one and the same salvation which is concerned with the total redemption of man.'[11] Social involvement may be the occasion and the means for evangelization. The radical, self-sacrificial giving of ourselves in the service of our fellow men is often a most effective way of commending the Gospel. The work of Mother Theresa in Calcutta is known to all. Does not this work in itself commend the Gospel? In the South Asian context, Christian involvement in leprosy work, in refugee relief, in providing education and medical care for the poor, are all effective ways of commending the Gospel. In the Sind, for instance, the evangelization of poor Hindū tribes has meant not only their conversion to Christianity but development of a wholly new community which is gradually being made aware about its rights and duties as Christians and citizens. The emergence of such a community is in itself a commendation of the Gospel.

CRESR attempts to make a distinction between pre-evangelism and evangelism. Pre-evangelism may take the form of social development and involvement and this may make conditions more favourable for evangelism.[12] The present writer believes that if the term evangelization is used, the other two terms are rendered superfluous. Evangelization may begin among a particular people with the arrival of Gospel values embodied in faithful Christian care and service, or it may begin with the proclamation of the *Kerygma* followed by 'love in action'. Evangelization is the exposure of an individual or a group of people to the demands of the Gospel and their gradual transformation as a result of this exposure. Evangelization in its truest sense would affect every area of life.

Teaching

The pastoral ministry of the Church underpins all other work, and it is the teaching ministry of the Church which forms the hard core of the pastoral ministry. St. Paul tells us that the gift of teaching is one of the gifts of the Holy Spirit for the building up of Christ's Church.[13] The teaching ministry of the Church finds expression in nearly every aspect of their corporate life: in the various house groups, at the fellowship and Bible Study meetings, at the various young people's meetings, in preaching and in involvement with various Christian and non-Christian organizations. It is biblically based, but attempts to relate the teaching of the Scriptures to the context. Recurring themes include an understanding of Islām in relation to the Bible: the role of a Christian minority in an Islāmic state; contextualization of life-style, worship and theology; the integrity of the Scriptures; the importance of the sacraments and the need for true interior change as opposed to mere outward legalism, etc. Teaching activity takes place in three languages: English, *Urdū* and *Punjābī*, and encompasses all social classes.

The teaching ministry of the Church is hermeneutical. The Church is called upon to interpret the Scriptures and Christian doctrine to each generation and to each culture. To do this effectively, Christian teachers need to be aware of both the milieux of the Bible and their own particular economic, political and cultural setting.

The teaching ministry is, however, more than being aware of

both these horizons. Authentic hermeneutical activity enables them to 'meet'. It brings the challenge and the promise of the Bible to bear on our contemporary situation. It is, primarily, making it possible for people to discover the Gospel: to realize its implications for themselves at all levels: personal, domestic and social; and to encourage application of Gospel values in every area of life.

> 'Not everyone who says to me, "Lord, Lord", shall enter the Kingdom of heaven, but only he who does the will of my Father who is in heaven' (Matt. 7:21).

CHAPTER 10

The Church of Pākistān Tomorrow: Hopes and Fears*

'He who has not been slain is not of our Tribe' (*Naẓīrī*).

The life of the Church of Pākistān is lived out today in a context which is becoming more and more difficult. There is cause for concern, and even for fear. The ordinary Christian lives out his life in a context of suffering, deprivation and discrimination (the most popular of the Psalms in *Punjābī* are those which deal with suffering and patience in adversity, e.g. 'I waited patiently for the Lord; he inclined to me and heard my cry'; Psalm 40:1). It would be easy to be helpless and despairing in such a situation. The miracle of Christianity is that instead of despair and fatalism, the situation is shot through with hope. It is in this spirit of hope that we begin an appraisal of various aspects of the Church's corporate life, and in humility, with a deep consciousness of God's overruling providence, offer certain suggestions about directions which the Church of Pākistān might take in the future.

1. A Vision of Church Union

Discussion of the nature of Church union in Pākistān must be in the more general context of ecumenical dialogue worldwide. There

*Paper prepared for a consultation between the COP and its partners, April 1985.

are many models of Christian unity ranging from institutional integration, to mutual recognition of ministries and sacraments.[1] What kind of Church union do we have in Pākistān? What kind of Church union do we want for the future, recognizing that our union is incomplete at the moment?

Church union in our context should be modelled on the collegial and communal pattern where the Bishops and their dioceses act together after mutual consultation (both informally and at Synodical level) on matters affecting the whole Church.[2] At the same time, each diocese and its bishop is autonomous (though not independent) in ordering its own affairs according to the constitution of the Church of Pākistān. Checks and balances are, however, necessary within the episcopate, in order to prevent the emergence of the (erroneously termed) 'Ignatian' bishop. Our models for ordering society are generally feudal in origin, and if episcopal autonomy is emphasized at the expense of collegiality and communality, there is the danger that we will end up with an absolutist, monarchical episcopate. Synodical government, episcopal collegiality, the principle of accountability and relationships with the worldwide Church, are necessary checks to balance an autonomous episcopate.

The significant achievement of the full interchange of ministries and full communion with each other as a means of drawing the different traditions together is not fully appreciated. In several dioceses, clergy from one tradition now minister in churches which have their origins in another tradition. In other dioceses, the bishop comes from a tradition other than the one dominant in the diocese! Large numbers of Christians have got used to receiving the sacraments at the hands of clergy who belong to traditions other than their own. There is a common interest in liturgical renewal, and a common recognition of the Eucharist as an event central in the Church's life and mission.

Centralized administration is desirable only insofar as it enables the Synod to function as a general supervisory body. A well-organized secretariat providing support for the various Synodical bodies to meet and circulate information would be helpful. A top-heavy superstructure, directly responsible for the mission and ministry of the Church, is not desirable. Bureaucracy kills local initiative, is cumbersome and too far removed from the situation on the ground to be able to take initiatives on its own. Our fear is that the Church in this respect will simply reflect society at large. In a heavily centralized situation, there is the danger that society's feudal models will be imported into the Church: centralization will become an occasion for dispensing patronage and privilege. Thus, power, instead of being dispersed throughout the whole Church, will become unacceptably concentrated.

The development of centralized services whose role is advisory rather than executive would be useful, for example in the fields of education, health, community development and theological education. The appropriate development of existing Synodical organs (such as the Theological Commission), would be one way of achieving such a goal. Inter-diocesan sharing of resources and experience would be another way to avoid duplicating effort.

A degree of centralization in theological education is necessary. A central Church of Pākistān theological college avoids unnecessary duplication of scarce resources in theological education, and creates an environment which encourages the evolution of common COP theological and liturgical traditions. Such a tradition should, however, be open to constructive criticism, renewal and development.

Where should such a college be situated? Eighty percent of the Christian population of the country is in the province of the *Punjāb*, which is also the geographical centre of the country. A location in the *Punjāb* is, therefore, desirable in some respects. Other locations have, however, been suggested. There is no objection to these in principle provided that the decisions of the Theological Commission which have been confirmed by the Synod Executive are respected. These include, inter-alia, the complete independence of the college (as an organ of the Synod) from the structures of the diocese in which it is situated. The college should reflect the nature of the Church of Pākistān, and there should be a balance between the different traditions as far as teaching staff is concerned. The leadership and make-up of the staff should be largely national, though expatriates should be welcome especially where they can provide otherwise unavailable expertize.[3] The different dioceses continue to have the primary responsibility for theological education in their own territories, and the continued existence of small diocesan institutions such as the one at Karachi cannot be ruled out. The tension between North and South on the question of the location of the proposed national institution may only be resolved by having two regional institutions, one in the south at Karachi, Hyderabad or Quetta, and the other in the North at Multan, Faisalabad, Raiwind, Lahore or Rawalpindi.

Certain theological programmes (such as Theological Education by Extension), and non-residential ordination courses are best run by the dioceses themselves, which should be enabled and encouraged to mount such programmes. Flourishing training programmes in some dioceses is an encouraging sign. The Diocese of Multan has had such a programme for many years, which is development-orientated. The Diocese of Lahore have initiated a modular programme on theological education for graduates and, most recently, the Diocese of Raiwind have begun a programme of TEE. If the present level of pastoral care is to be maintained and improved, many different models of theological training will have to be developed and employed throughout the Church. Some candidates for the ordained ministry are at a stage in their professional and domestic lives where they cannot easily go to a traditional training college. Some wish to remain in their employment and yet are called to the ordained ministry. Are such vocations to be regarded as deficient?

The ministry of women is another area of urgent concern. An adequate number of women in the ministry is necessary, especially in Pākistān where a certain amount of social segregation is still to be found. The pastoral work of the Church among women is severely hampered by the small number of women in the ministry. Women should certainly be immediately ordained to a diaconal ministry in accordance with the primitive custom of the Church. Deaconesses have existed in the constituent parts of the Church of Pākistān before and it is now time for the whole Church to affirm their ministry in this way. The question of their ordination to the presbyterate and episcopate should not be decided unilaterally by the Church of Pākistān. We should actively promote the emergence of a common mind on the issue among Churches with a historic three-fold ministry with whom we are in full communion. Also, we should be praying for a common mind on the issue in the Universal Church. Debate on the question should be encouraged in the Church of Pākistān. Provision should be made for the training of women in any scheme for theological eduation which is brought to Synod or to Diocesan councils.

The fundamental problem with the functioning of the Synod is that we are committed to a democratic polity in a communal Church, which is in turn situated in a society where decisions are made by consensus. The problem with decisions by consensus is that the process is too slow. Yet, any attempt to speed it up is regarded as disruptive and not conducive to the general good. Differences of opinion on matters of principle are often taken as opposition to a person or a group. The difficulty with universal adult franchize in a communal Church is that those who are elected to offices in the Church are not necessarily its most committed members. This has repercussions in every area of the Church's life, but especially when elections are held to a vacant see or for officers of a diocesan council or synod. Without opting for a 'sectarian' alternative, it is nevertheless highly desirable that there should be doctrinal and ethical criteria for those who would seek membership of any council in the Church. Also, the period between notification of an election and the election itself should be sharply reduced to avoid canvassing, corruption and manipulation. Ultimately it is only a sober, committed and learned ministry which will prevent abuse of our polity. Ministerial formation, from selection through to ordination, must ensure that only those with a true vocation are ordained and entrusted with pastoral care. The role of the diocesan ordinary is of crucial importance in this respect.

2. Relations with Other Churches within the Country

The Church should reaffirm its wholehearted commitment to ecumenism and to the National Council of Churches in Pākistān. There have been tensions in this relationship, but despite these, the National Council of Churches is a vital organ which can further the work of Christian unity in this land. Relations with the Roman Catholic Church are somewhat uneven; in some places and among certain groups and individuals they are very warm, in other places they are formal at best. In some places there is a regular exchange of ministry and even a limited kind of intercommunion, in others *communicatio in sacris* is conspicuous by its absence. We should reiterate our desire to seek closer understanding and relations with the Roman Church, not only on issues of justice, peace and communal rights, but also in theology; particularly, as it relates to the doctrine of the ministry and sacraments. Belief in these matters in the Church of Pākistān is closer to Rome than in any of the Churches of the Reformation. We should make clear our desire that the Roman Catholic Church should seek membership of the National Council of Churches in Pākistān. Our desire for unity with the non-episcopal churches should be based on the provisions of the Lambeth Quadrilateral and the Plan for Church Union, which brought the Church of Pākistān and the Church of North India into existence.[4]

The centrality of Scripture, creeds, dominical sacraments and episcopacy need not be accepted in an uncritical spirit. We affirm the authority of Scripture in the Church, while recognizing the need to study the origins of Scripture in the various cultures which gave birth to the documents. We must study also the forms of narrative in Scripture and their evolution, the relationship of

Scripture to other contemporary documents and above all, the problems of hermeneutics, so that Scripture is interpreted to contemporary society as a meaningful proclamation of Judgement and Salvation.

The creeds are the formulations of scriptural faith in a particular *Sitz im Leben*, requiring reinterpretation and reformulation in our own context.[5] The sacraments, too, are not to be regarded as magical rites for the superstitious, but neither are they to be regarded as merely symbolic. They are to be understood as means of divine grace as expressions of corporate 'openness' to the divine initiative. Episcopacy in particular is not to be interpreted in rigid absolutist terms, but as an ancient (and agreeable to Scripture) form of Church government which has withstood the test of time. The pastoral and caring role of a bishop is to be emphasized over and against the traditional understanding of his role as ruler.

A possible bone of contention between Churches is the agreement on comity which took place soon after partition, and much before Church Union. This agreement divided the country between the different Churches and related mission bodies, such that there would be no overlap in the work of the bodies party to the agreement (excepting cities with a population of over 300,000). One difficulty with this agreement is that the Roman Catholic Church was not a party to it. Therefore, if comity rules are allowed to stand as they are, the Roman Catholic Church will be the sole Church which can claim to be national in scope. Also, the 'open areas', (cities with a certain population), are defined without respect to the fact that the Christian population may be concentrated in cities with a smaller population. The likelihood of Christians in these cities coming from different traditions is obviously greater. Lastly, the rules make no provision for the fact that the predominant tradition in a certain area may be a dying one without reasonable hope of renewal. Should other churches in such a case, simply watch the demise of Christianity in the area?

The Constitution of the Church of Pākistān envisages a territorial Church, divided into dioceses and pastorates which, in theory at least, should cover the whole of the national territory. In other words, there can be nowhere in Pākistān which is not under jurisdiction of some diocesan bishop.[6] It is, therefore, incumbent upon the Church of Pākistān to maintain a pastoral presence wherever its members are to be found, and to create a missionary presence where they are not to be found. This should be done sensitively, without undue offence and without 'sheep stealing' from other Churches.

3. Relations with Churches Outside Pākistān and Regional and International Ecclesial Bodies

a) We reaffirm our critical commitment to bodies like the Christian Conference of Asia and the World Council of Churches. They are still the only viable bodies whose main aim is to promote the unity of Christian Churches, and whose membership ranges from the ancient oriental Churches to the newest independent Churches. There are, however, serious imbalances in the ecumenical movement and the bureaucracy often have too high a profile. Successive Church of Pākistān delegates to ecumenical assemblies have, for example, pointed out that while certain powers are singled out for criticism regarding their commitment to human rights (so far so good), others, whose commitment to human rights is at least as obscure, are not mentioned at all! We welcome the present prophetic trend in the Church but the prophecy must be directed at all human beings, at all countries and all blocs. The proclamation of God's Judgement cannot be selective. We recognize that different methods may be employed *vis à vis* different powers, but there can be no silence.

We welcome the Ecumenical Movement's involvement with justice and peace issues, and we recognize it as part of the biblical mandate for our generation. However, we would also plead for a recognition that *human sinfulness* is at the root of *human sinned-againstness*. The poor are not simply sinned against but are, in turn, sinful in terms of their own relationships with God and neighbour. We are committed to struggle for structures in society which will make injustice less possible, which will ensure a greater distribution of wealth and which will enable power-sharing. At the same time we are deeply aware that all social structures are vitiated by human sin and cannot be a substitute for the Kingdom of God.

We fully endorse the programme to encourage 'peoples' theologies' particularly in Asia, Africa and Latin America. We are painfully conscious, however, that at least some such theologies are in fact formulated by Western-trained theologians and are often founded on radical critical methods developed in the West. It is true that the World Council of Churches and the Christian Conference of Asia have of late begun to pay more attention to non-formal theological expression and this trend is to be welcomed.[7] Bishop Newbigin has made a perceptive observation that rich resources of faith remain inaccessible to the ecumenical movement because they are in languages and forms with which members of the movement are not familiar. Genuine 'peoples' theologies', however, are likely to be expressed precisely in such forms and languages.[8] We should encourage any effort which seeks to make these resources available to the worldwide Church.

b) Let us now consider relations with the ecclesial traditions from which the uniting Churches have come: we seek to maintain and to strengthen our fellowship with all these traditions, and we particularly welcome our relations of full communion with these Churches and with other Churches with whom the uniting Churches were in communion before Union.

We express our disappointment, however, with a paper recently circulated by the Anglican Consultative Council on Episcopal Churches written by the Revd. Professor Henry Chadwick. This paper has the effect of reducing the status of the united Churches *vis à vis* the Anglican communion, and does not fully recognize the fact that there is a strong Anglican component in the united Churches, which did not anticipate such a reduction in status. Our token membership of the Anglican Consultative Council (one bishop) is again a source of disappointment and frustration. Even more surprising is the complete exclusion of united Church representatives from bilateral dialogues investigating the possibilities of wider Union. This is precisely the area where our representatives might have the most meaningful contribution to make! Most painful in this context is the exclusion from both the Anglican-Roman Catholic International Commissions (ARCIC) I and II. At the 1978 Lambeth Conference the united Churches were represented by only one bishop for each of these Churches. This has now been increased to 20 per cent of the episcopal bench. One of the ways in which the Anglican communion has been defined is that it is a fellowship of Churches in communion with the See of Canterbury. On this basis, invitations to Lambeth should be sent to all diocesan bishops of Churches in communion with Canterbury. Recent initiatives taken by the Anglican Consultative Council to include the membership of united Churches in the councils of Anglicanism are to be warmly welcomed.

The difficulty with the Lutheran Churches is the state-orientation of many of them, which makes exchange of ministries difficult. Their character as national Churches makes changes in their structure dependent on state legislation, which causes frustration among their partners. There has been little theological dialogue with the Lutheran tradition and the united Churches have not been involved in the several very significant Roman Catholic-Lutheran and Anglican-Lutheran conversations that have taken place. Relations with the Methodist and the Presbyterian traditions are reasonably warm, but there is great room for expansion especially in the fields of theological discussions on wider ecumenism; dialogue concerning the nature and mission of the Church; approaches to the other world faiths; education and development.

In recent years, many of the COP's partner Churches and agencies, while stressing the need for relating to the Church of Pākistān as a whole, have been channelling considerable amounts of aid through bodies which do not seem to be accountable in any way to the Church of Pākistān, or even its dioceses. How far is this consistent with the aim to relate in a more coordinated and meaningful way with the Church of Pākistān?

c) In accordance with the Constitution (ch. XVI, art. 4), the Church of Pākistān continues to be in full communion with all those Churches which were in communion with the uniting Churches at the time of Union. The Church should reaffirm its full communion with the wider episcopal family including the Old Catholic Church and in particular the Mar Thoma Syrian Church in India. Mar Thoma bishops were regularly used in consecrations of bishops in the Church of India, Pākistān, Burma and Ceylon, and were used by the Church of North India at the time of the inauguration of Church Union. Their presence at such consecrations has brought the much valued Eastern episcopal tradition into the Anglican and united Church traditions. It is highly desirable that Old Catholic and Mar Thoma bishops be invited to participate in Church of Pākistān consecrations.

d) As a Church living in an Islāmic polity, the Church needs to develop relations with the Oriental Orthodox and Eastern Catholic Churches, especially those which have maintained a long Christian witness in Muslim lands. The Church can learn from them how to survive in an Islāmic context. It can emulate their positive contribution in this respect, and learn from their mistakes.[9] Some of the Church's partners (such as the Church Missionary Society who have a long history of relationships with such Churches), can help the Church of Pākistān to create close links with these Churches. Interchange need not be merely from the sub-continent to the UK or from the Middle East to the UK, but also may be from the Middle East to the sub-continent and vice-versa.

e) Relations with Eastern Orthodox also need to be developed, as many of them live in Islāmic societies. Many sections of Orthodoxy have recognized the validity of Anglican Orders (one source of the COP's Orders), and it is desirable to begin conversations with them. The difficulty created by the ordination of women in parts of the Anglican communion, as far as Anglican-Eastern Orthodox dialogue is concerned, does not arise in the same way for the COP, and so real progress may be possible. Interchanges, especially in the field of theological education, would be greatly beneficial and should be facilitated. The Church of Pākistān can learn a great deal from Orthodox spirituality which, often developed in difficult social situations, is analagous to our own today.

4. Beyond Suspicion: Relations with Parachurch Groups

Relations between the Church of Pākistān and parachurch groups have often been those of mutual suspicion. Parachurch groups have usually perceived the Church as hidebound and uninterested in new initiatives in evangelization, whereas the Church has seen parachurch groups as too dependent on outside support and disruptive.

Certain problems need to be faced straight away if a more creative relationship is to develop. Some parachurch bodies have moved into Pākistān without first seeking a relationship with some part of Christ's Church in Pākistān. Sometimes the wisdom of what they are doing in the country is questionable and the long-range effects on the Church of 'pioneer' ministries is insufficiently considered. The attitude, 'Let's do it and be thrown out' is characteristic of such movments. Many parachurch movements 'cream-off' the best young people, who otherwise might have been available for ministry in the Church of Pākistān or in other Churches. Only a few parachurch bodies, such as the Pākistān Fellowship of Evangelical Students, attempt to 'feed' their workers back into the Church's ministry. The ministry of certain para-Church groups, however, has been a source of renewal for the Church. The Church must affirm such ministries, and where the presence of a parachurch group has been shown to benefit the community, it should be strengthened and supported in its task.

Indigenous parachurch groups of lay Christians committed to the fulfilment of certain ministries in evangelism, discipling and development have also emerged. Where their work is beneficial, they must be enabled to fulfil their task. It is the role of a diocesan bishop to enable the work of mission to proceed within his diocese and not merely within diocesan structures. The identification and support of community and small group initiatives should be an important part of episcopal responsibility.

While affirming the reality of ministry by parachurch groups, the Church of Pākistān does not accept any ecclesiology which attempts to project parachurch groups as Churches (this is sometimes done by saying that parachurch groups are Churches in mission). Nor does the Church of Pākistān recognize the attempts to create Churches on ethnic, caste or cultural lines as evangelical.

Christians from similar backgrounds, can meet for fellowship, Bible-study and worship, but such groups are not to be elevated to the status of a Church. In the New Testament, the Church is a gathered community of diverse kinds of people who have been made one in Christ (Acts 6; Gal. 2; Col. 3), and it should be our vision to integrate all kinds of people into Christ's Church in Pākistān. We need a renewed commitment among clergy and people in the Church of Pākistān to accept people from backgrounds other than their own into their fellowship.[10]

5. Relations with Islām

The Church of Pākistān finds itself in an increasingly Islāmic polity, and efforts must be made to adjust to such a polity in a positive way. Islāmicization has produced a range of situations which directly affect the Christian community. For the Christian minority, a new socio-legal situation has been produced which needs to be evaluated and to which a response must be made. Important changes have taken place concerning separate electorates and the Law of Evidence. Christians may now vote only for Christians in local, provincial and national elections and the number of Christian seats is fixed. In the case of national and provincial elections, the whole nation or province is the Christian candidate's constituency. Any number of candidates can stand, and those who get the most votes up to a fixed number (4 in the national and up to 5 in the provincial assembly), stand elected. This method results in serious imbalances. For example, most of the Christian population of the country lives in the *Punjāb*. Thus, all Christians elected for the National Assembly will be from the *Punjāb*, and the Christians in other provinces are effectively disenfranchized.

In elections to the Provincial Assembly, those parts of the province which have a large Christian population will be heavily represented whilst others are left disenfranchized. As the Christian has no vote in his local constituency, he has no guarantee of a hearing from his local member. The Christian minority is not satisfied with the number of seats allotted to it *vis à vis* other minorities. It has been suggested that Churches should jointly undertake a census of the Christian population: the matter is controversial as there are advantages and disadvantages in undertaking such a venture.

The Government claims that separate electorates have been introduced to give minorities effective representation at all levels of government. This is to be welcomed, but it needs to be pointed out that such representation is possible without depriving minorities of the right to vote for the members of the constituency where they reside. The method of the double-vote or that of reserved seats (as for women) are two ways of achieving this representation.

The Law of Evidence is another area of grave concern. The law (based on the *Sharīʿah*) is framed in such a way as to jeopardize the acceptability of minorities as witnesses in any matter which involves a Muslim. This leaves minorities in a very exposed state. The Government claims that the law will not be used to put minorities at a disadvantage, but why is it thought necessary to frame a law which seems to militate against all canons of natural justice? Extremists may use such laws against minorities in the future. Other laws, too, have been promulgated which seem to go even beyond the bounds of *Sharīʿah* in affecting the status of minorities. The *Sharīʿah* allows a certain freedom to minorities, leaving particular matters to be decided by their own courts. The present laws, however, treat minorities on a par with Muslims.[11] Some extremist voices are advocating even greater restrictions, creating a climate of uncertainty for religious minorities.

Fear has also been created in other groups concerning their rights. Women's rights are a prime example: the problem is analogous to that being faced by religious minorities. Christians should stand for the equality of all before the law, and defend guarantees given by the Constitution. Certain Christian organizations (such as the NCCP and the YWCA), have taken a principled stand on the issue.

The question of freedom of religion requires careful consideration. At the time of writing, we are thankful that there are no significant restrictions in the profession and propagation of Christianity, but such is not the case with other religious minorities. Here, too, Christians must work for the implementation of constitutional guarantees.

Ecumenical bodies (such as the Christian Study Centre, Rawalpindi), local churches and individuals are engaged in continuous dialogue with Muslims of all kinds of theological persuasion. There is real dialogue with fundamentalist Muslims on theological as well as socio-political issues. There is dialogue with more liberal Muslims on the question of human rights, the creation of a just economic and social order, the nature of religious belief and its relevance to contemporary society and a list of other topics. Then, there is dialogue with *Ṣūfī* (or mystical) Islām (especially the reformists among them) on the nature of religious experience, Muslim-Christian interaction in the area of spirituality, the relation between law and grace, etc.

The Church of Pākistān must affirm all existing dialogue and must encourage it within its own structures. There is a need to conscientize the laity such that effective dialogue can be sustained at the work place and in the neighbourhood. The prior training of clergy in Christian-Muslim relations is an urgent priority in order to achieve this goal. Ordination courses should include substantial components on Islāmic studies and in-service training should also give due weight to this subject. This is already done in some areas, but it needs to be greatly expanded. Experts who can advise the Government (directly or through Christian legislators) on issues concerning Muslim-Christian relations need to be trained. The limited scale of the present programme needs expansion. Without such expertize, Christians are left at the mercy of uninformed and, sometimes, self-seeking spokesmen.

6. New Directions

The vision is of dynamic Church unity: there is need to stress function rather than structure. Although this is controversial, it is difficult to see how the mission of Christ can proceed in any other way. Certain structures are necessary, however, for Christians to express their unity in mission. Some already exist within the COP, others exist outside it, others need to be developed. Christian leaders should advocate a radical shift from the traditional obsession with property and institutions towards an emphasis on human and community-related development. The 'Small is Beautiful' concept is to be commended in mission thinking. Small groups gathering together to bring about meaningful social change on a local scale are to be encouraged. Such community projects should not be capital intensive. There is no denying the need for property and for comparatively large institutions, nor should the past ministry of large institutions be denied, but new initiatives must be taken in community-related development.

A new understanding of *episcopē* as enabling the whole Church, and especially communities, groups and individuals, to take genuinely fresh initiatives in mission is to be commended. Such an understanding is bound to be in tension with traditional understandings, but this is a necessary and, ultimately, creative tension.

It is to be hoped that the Christian community as a whole, and the Church of Pākistān in particular, will move away from preoccupation with its own safety and its own rights and will become more and more concerned with the safety, rights and prosperity of all fellow-citizens in this country and with the wider human family beyond, especially with the poor, with those oppressed by exploitative structures, with those without freedom of religion, and with the spiritually-lost, whether rich or poor.

> 'O God, who on this day, through thine only-begotten Son, hast conquered death, and thrown open to us the gate of ever-lasting life, give effect by thine aid to our desires, which thou dost anticipate and inspire. Through the same Jesus Christ, thy Son, who liveth and reigneth with thee in the Unity of the Holy Spirit, ever one God, world without end.'
>
> [Ancient form of the Collect for the feast of the Resurrection].

Part III
Faith in Dialogue

Introduction

Dialogue, like encounter, is clearly one of those words which has been over-used of late. Some might say it has been misused. In itself, it is a word to which no Christian should take exception as it is used in the New Testament. In the New Testament it is sometimes used in the context of inter-faith encounter! (Acts 17:2; 18:4; 19:8) In such passages the word is variously translated, ranging from 'disputation' to 'discussion'. The sense of the word is rendered by something like 'discussion for the sake of persuasion'.[1] In recent usage, however, it has come to mean more than this. It can signify an attitude of sympathy towards those of other faith. It may be promoted to increase understanding and cooperation in matters affecting the various communities. It may also be understood as deepening the Christian's perception of his own faith. While affirming these contemporary perceptions of inter-faith dialogue, the Christian, in consonance with the New Testament, will want also to stress the role of dialogue as 'a medium of authentic witness'.[2] Such witness, however, must be preceded by careful listening to one's partner's point of view; the witness itself must be carried out in love and humility and the Christian should be prepared to learn from the experience.

The emergence of a religiously plural world, with greatly increased possibilities of inter-faith and multi-faith encounters, makes dialogue between people of different faiths extremely important. This is so not only for religious reasons, although these are very important, but also for development of a genuinely free and just society which fosters mutual tolerance and respect between groups and individuals with different beliefs.

Dialogue may be carried out officially by international bodies (such as the World Council of Churches), or by regional bodies (such as the Christian Conference of Asia) and their counterparts, representing other religious traditions. At a national level, it may be carried out by councils of Churches or by ecumenical study centres. Voluntary bodies at international, regional and national level may also become involved in dialogue and, indeed, may be established specifically for dialogue. The World Conference on Religion for Peace is an example of such a body at an international level. Other such bodies exist at regional or national level. Dialogue at these levels may be bilateral, for example, between those of the Christian tradition and one other tradition, or it may be multilateral, i.e., between people of different religious traditions.

In addition to these 'structured' forms of dialogue, there are more informal ways to conduct dialogue. Christian 'presence' centres in different parts of the world maintain dialogue with those of another tradition on the basis of neighbourliness. In the same way those of another tradition may maintain a 'presence' in a society with a dominant Christian tradition. We may say, therefore, that dialogue of this kind is carried out wherever one religious tradition maintains a presence in an area where another tradition is dominant. The most meaningful kind of inter-faith dialogue perhaps is that between neighbours, friends and relations. It is here that particularly difficult questions of belief and practices are discussed in an atmosphere of trust and commitment to each other which is not affected by the outcome of the discussion.

For the Christian, dialogue raises a whole number of questions which lead him to reflect on his own faith and on its relation to that of his partner in dialogue. What is offered in the following chapters is the result of some of this reflection.

CHAPTER 11

Christianity in Relationship to Other Faiths*

Father Knox of Oxford used to say that the only effect of Comparative Religions was to make people comparatively religious! Similarly that great Baptist preacher C. H. Spurgeon once said that in his opinion there may be comparative religions but that Christianity was not one of them! When a young man asked for advice about his approaching ministry he is reported to have said, 'in the first instance preach Christ, in the second instance preach Christ and in the third instance preach Christ!' A similar view of the Christian approach to Islām is expressed in the following excerpt from a letter which appeared in a Christian periodical:

> 'The Christian approach in the Bible, the King of Kings' Regulations, is quite unequivocal. No one comes to God as Father except by Christ because He alone has removed the sin barrier by an efficacious atonement, the Sacrifice (*Qurbānī*) which God accepts (John 14:6; Ephes. 2:12–18, Heb. 10:10; John 1:29, etc.). We claim an inspired book and a Superior person to any other Prophet (Heb. 1:1–14): the one who claimed 'he who has seen me has seen the Father'. The only way I know to approach Muslims is to let each have his say and trust God to reveal the Truth'.

Such an attitude towards other religions is best articulated by Hendrik Kraemer, a neo-orthodox theologian. Kraemer holds that the Christian faith is unique, God's final self-disclosure. The other

*Paper prepared for the Oxford Council of Churches, 1977.

religions of the world are the inventions of a fallen mankind and are inevitably vitiated by the total depravity of man. God finds them guilty of the sin of pride as they claim to understand the nature of ultimate reality through human effort and do not realize the necessity of grace.[1]

Views on the relationship of Christianity to other faiths are often polarized; the other extreme is represented by the *Radhakrishnan* school of 'indifferentism'. This holds that Christianity is merely a 'form' of religion and quite on a par with other 'forms' of religion. John Hick comments that there needs to be a 'Copernican revolution' in the field of religious studies just as there has been in the sciences. This revolution would enable us to see that no one religion is at the centre but that all together form a whole. Each religion has only a part of the truth and needs the others to complement it. The different religions of the world are seen as the expression of one universal religion.[2] Those who adopt this attitude sometimes speak of the religions of the world as 'denominations' of a universal or perennial religion.

An alternative view is that there is an element of truth in both positions. Christianity as the Gospel, i.e. as the unique and definitive self-disclosure of God in Christ, is over and above the religions of the world including the Christian religion. On the other hand, Christianity as the expression of the human response to the Gospel in cultural and literary terms is a religion like other religions. The Christian religion and the Gospel are not the same thing:-

> 'Christianity is a human answer to the Gospel, to God's Word in Jesus Christ. As a human, earthly, answer Christianity is always subject to the rubric: "Not that I have already obtained" (Phil. 3:12). It is not what it is intended to be . . . Christianity is both one religion among many and a unique phenomenon. It is a religion among many religions insofar as it comes under God's judgement. And it is a unique phenomenon insofar and as soon as it is a witness for the Word, the Gospel, God's revelation in Christ . . .'[3]

In the same way it may be said that there are elements in most cultures and faith-systems which are responses to God's self-disclosure in the natural order, in conscience and in religious experience. It has to be understood, however, that such responses would be seriously distorted due to human sin. The Christian response may be termed 'special' only because it is seen as a response to God's unique and definitive self-disclosure in Jesus Christ. It should be noted that the view that religions as human systems are vitiated by the depravity of man would apply to the Christian religion as well. It also needs pointing out that non-

Christian religions do not all claim to be the product of human effort alone, within many of them there is a profound consciousness that they are responses to divine initiative—whether communicated through messengers or communicated directly by touching the human heart. There *is* then a self-disclosure of God among the followers of many non-Christian religions (this is admitted even by Kraemer). Such a revelation may or may not be mediated by the religion concerned. It could, for example, be experienced quite outside the framework of a particular religious system or even in opposition to it. The response to this revelation, however, is always corrupted because of the Fall.

How is the self-disclosure of God in Christ linked to his self-disclosure in the non-Christian cultures and religious systems of the world? One answer is in the doctrine of Fulfilment. Just as Christ fulfilled the Old Testament so also he fulfils the best in other religions of the World. Although Christ's fulfilment of the Old Testament was subsequent in time to the O.T. revelation, this need not be the case with the other religions. Islām arose after the incarnation and yet it may be fulfilled by Christ if he meets its deepest needs and aspirations.

There are two ways in which the Gospel may be seen as 'fulfilling' the best in non-Christian religions. First, basic mythical hopes and aspirations may be seen as 'recapitulated' in the person of Christ. For example, the hope that the deity would become incarnate is found in nearly all major religions: the doctrine of the *Avatars* in the religions of Indian origin (e.g. the story of *Vishnu's* incarnation as *Krishna* in Hindūism), the doctrine of Divine Presence in the *Guru* (whether human or a book) among the Sikhs and the doctrine of *Nūr-Al-Muḥammadiyya* and *Haqīqat-Al-Muḥammadiyya* which treats *Muḥammad* as divine. *Ṣūfī* mystics also sometimes refer to one's spiritual director (*pīr*) in incarnational terms. In these cases the doctrine is either founded on legend, like the *Krishna* Story, (Hindūs will often emphasize the lack of the importance of history in their tradition), or it is developed contrary to the explicit teaching of the leader (e.g. *Muḥammad*), or it is developed in a moment of mystical passion. The significant element in these doctrines is the longing to know God in a way which the senses can comprehend. Not as an impersonal absolute, nor as a personal but utterly transcendent being, but as someone very close to man. The presence of God in Christ in the full light of history 'recapitulates' all these hopes and aspirations in one historical event. The term 'recapitulation' is first used by the early Church Father, Irenaeus, in his development of the doctrine of Christ as the New Adam in whom humanity is recreated.

The theme of sacrifice is also common in the religious systems of the world. The primaeval order is seen as disrupted by some catastrophe and a return to the original order is desperately needed. This return is very often effected through sacrifice.[4] The death of Christ has been seen in the Christian tradition as a sacrifice which fulfils the hope expressed in the sacrifices of the Mosaic Covenant (which may be seen as types or shadows of Christ's sacrifice). In the same way, can Christ's sacrifice be seen as a fulfilment of the hope of reconciliation and wholeness which is expressed in the sacrifices in other religions? The conscious obedience to death of the Last Adam reconciles us with God the Father. The Father who has been spurned again and again by the fully conscious disobedience of the First Adam. God's eternal suffering, sacrificing love is revealed fully in his 'provision' of his Son as the perfect sacrifice who restores wholeness to man and reconciles him to his Creator. Christ does for man what he cannot do for himself.

The movement begun by the heretic Marcion proved to be sterile as it did not relate the work and person of Christ to the Old Testament. Jesus Christ was taken in isolation from the rest of Salvation History (as he sometimes is in contemporary theology) and little sense could be made of his work. The Incarnation was seen not as the culmination of a progressive revelation through history but as the singular penetration by a good God into a world created by an evil demon.[5] Similarly, it is often held, it is sterile to preach Christ among followers of different religions without trying to relate Christ's work to the aspirations expressed in the myth and ritual of these religions.

When the comparison is between two 'historical' religions like Islām and Christianity, then fulfilment is seen more in the character of Christ as the ideal messenger of God. This reality may be seen in the moral excellence of his teaching and the moral perfection of his life. It may be seen in the power displayed in his earthly ministry or in the glory of his resurrection. It is seen also in the perfect submission of the cross. Islām (which means submission) shows the need for a figure like Jesus. The task of the Christian is to make Muslims aware of Jesus. This can be done best by starting with the *Qur'ānic* account of Jesus (which has a Christology, though most of it is explained away by Muslim commentators) and developing it using the Gospels as source material. (Several lives of Christ, modelled on the *Diatessaron*, have appeared in certain languages spoken by Muslims, which use this way of introducing the figure of Christ to Muslims.) Many Muslims come to Christian faith because they find in Jesus the ideal that

Islām has set forth, but has been unable to supply.

The question of common prayer with adherents of other religions is a recurrent issue. For the 'indifferentist' school, there is no problem. Other religions are necessary complements to Christianity. No one religion is superior. But can one inspiration be the source of such diverse ideas? The reality and immortality of the soul are fundamental beliefs in Christianity and Islām, yet in Buddhism both are explicitly denied. Again, in Christianity, Judaism and Islām, the notion of a personal, transcendent God is fundamental; yet in philosophical Hindūism God is thought to be identical with the human self. In Peter Barnes' play *The Ruling Class* the following dialogue is recorded:

> Claire: How do you know you're . . . God?
> Earl of Gurney (a schizophrenic): Simple. When I pray to him I find I am talking to myself.[6]

In Barnes' play this may be the raving of a lunatic but the Hindū would be quite serious in saying something very similar, as would a certain type of Muslim mystic. For the Christian or the Muslim, prayer is an appeal to a mighty, benevolent being; for the Hindū it is an attempt at self-realization.

If other religions are regarded simply as idolatrous, then common worship with the representatives of other faiths is shunned. This attitude is not confined to ultra-fundamentalists but is also found among certain 'hard-line' neo-orthodox theologians. The Islāmic concept of God may be considered sublime but at the same time essentially idolatrous, as it is a product of the human mind. It has sometimes been called a 'conceptual idol'.

If Christianity is regarded as unique and yet related to other religions, then it may be possible to pray with members of other faiths even though the revelation contained in these faiths is not held to be adequate. Charles Marsh, an Evangelical who worked in the Chad (a predominantly Muslim country) for forty years, admits that on several occasions he prayed with individual Muslims and he thinks that the prayer was blessed. However, he believes that such prayer must be limited to very special cases, or the uniqueness of Christ will be compromised.

The problem with the inter-faith service is that it has to take place at the level of the lowest common denominator. The most distinctive features of each religion are excluded since they are not acceptable to the others. *Muḥammad's* role as mediator is excluded for the Muslim. Christ cannot be called upon to intercede before God for the Christians. Yet Christian worship has always been Christ-centred: 'For where two or three are gathered in my name, there am I in the midst of them' (Matt. 18:29). Again, 'Whatever you ask in my name, I will do it, that the Father may be glorified in the Son; if you ask anything in my name, I will do it' (John 14:13, 14). Christian prayers and the Eucharist are centred on Christ. The fundamental question for a Christian is whether worship can be meaningful without the name of Christ.[7]

It has been seen already how prayer with non-Christians can become a pastoral necessity. Sometimes it becomes necessary, in certain cultures, for Christians to join in acts of worship with those of other faiths (on occasions of national importance, for example). This can often be done without compromising Christian integrity. School assembly is another occasion when a Christian may feel it right to join in an act of worship with those of other faiths. Again, this can often be done without compromise. Such acts of worship do, however, take place at the level of the lowest common denominator and are, at best, only shadows of full Christian worship where Christ is at the centre. In no sense are such acts of worship a substitute for Christian worship. They may be carried out for pastoral reasons or to maintain a Christian presence but they do not replace authentic Christian worship.

CHAPTER 12

Christian Theology for Inter-Faith Dialogue*

'Up vistaed hopes, I sped, and shot, precipitated,
Adown Titanic glooms of Chasmèd fears,
From those strong Feet that followed, followed after.
But with unhurrying chase, and unperturbèd pace,
Deliberate speed, majestic instancy.
They beat, and a voice beat more instant than the feet—
'All things betray thee, who betrayest Me.'

Francis Thompson
The Hound of Heaven

'An old man was wandering around town
with a lamp in his hand saying,
"I am tired of hunters and beasts of prey, I seek a man!"
I said to him, "Such a one is not to be
found, we have sought him far."
He said, "That which is not to be
found, that is my desire!" '

Rūmī, from the *Dīwān-i-Shams-i-Tabrīz*

Inter-faith dialogue takes place in a context wider than the merely religious. It is neither simply an exchange of information aobut each others' religious beliefs, nor merely the 'swapping' of accounts of religious experience. Discussion about religious beliefs

*First published in *Towards a Theology of Inter-Faith Dialogue*, Anglican Consultative Council, London, 1986. Reprinted with permission.

and the recounting of paradigmatic religious experience are important aspects of dialogue, but they are not all of it. Inter-faith dialogue cannot proceed in isolation from the socio-political and economic conditions existing in the society where such dialogue is being carried out.

Religion, and in a plural situation the religion of the majority, tends to be a factor in the maintenance of the *status quo* and is indeed used to legitimize the oppression of minority and marginalized groups. In such a situation inter-faith dialogue must not be merely the scholarly exchange of information about each others' religion, nor must it be simply a discussion group of the mystically inclined: it must bring to the fore sharp and uncomfortable questions about the role of religion in society and must set the 'prophetic' against the merely 'cultic'. Muslims, for example, in dialogue with Christians justly raise issues such as the legitimation of racism in the name of the Bible in South Africa and in the Middle East.

Again, Christianity's historical encounter with Hindūism posed a sharp challenge to the very basis on which traditional Hindū society was organized. This challenge was significant in the reform and renewal of Hindūism in the 19th and 20th centuries.[1] In the Indian context, Casteism and its religious justification must form an item on the agenda of Christian-Hindū dialogue today.[2] In the same way, in dialogue with Muslims Christians will want to discuss what should be our common commitment to basic human rights, the protection of women's rights, and the rights of other powerless groups within the house of Islām; and Islām's contribution towards consensus regarding basic social justice in our world.

These aspects of Muslim-Christian dialogue are not extra to the agenda for inter-faith dialogue, but at the centre; they involve Muslim and Christian world-views, ideas on the nature of revelation, beliefs about divine ordering of society and many other matters central to both faith systems.[3]

It is important for the Anglican Communion (including the united Churches, the Mar Thoma Syrian Church, the Philippines Independent Church and the Old Catholics) to recognize the historical nature of inter-faith encounter. In some provinces, it is true, inter-faith encounter has only just begun but there are many others where it has been a fact of daily life for centuries. Anglicans in the Middle East, for example, can draw upon the vast resources of the ancient Churches to come to a realistic *modus vivendi* with Islām. Such resources, however, have to be used critically. The same accommodations and compromises which were forced on the ancient Churches need not be accepted today. Present conditions are somewhat different due to world concern for religious minorities, the presence of Muslim minorities in traditionally Christian countries and the Muslim insistence on freedom to practice *Da'wah* (invitation to Islām).

Different models for Muslim-Christian coexistence and dialogue are both desirable and available. One such model, for the Middle East, sees the future Christian Church as numerically small and politically powerless. Survival would depend upon not being seen as a threat to the major community and in establishing servant-structures in the Church which allow it to be seen as a serving and, therefore, necessary community.[4] Models which allow Christians to strive more actively for social and political emancipation within a secular system may be more appropriate elsewhere, such as in South East Asia. In the Indian sub-continent, the centuries-long experience of the St. Thomas Christians, their considerable integration into the Hindū social order and yet the maintenance of their distinctiveness are worthy of study.

Unfortunately, the Anglican theology of inter-faith dialogue has often been British specific.[5] Thus the comparative newness of plural society in Great Britain has been emphasized and the pioneering nature of inter-faith dialogue has been promoted. The specificity of the context, however, has led to a loss of historic consciousness. Such a loss is a loss for the British context as well as for the communion, and accounts for the fact that little attention is paid to the views of Asian, African and Latin American Christians resident in Britain in the formulation of such a theology. It has also resulted in insufficient attention to Churches and Christians in non-western plural situations.

Such situations are of several kinds:

1. Where Christians are a majority

These situations are very rarely taken into account. Examples are the Philippines in Asia, Ethiopia and (say) Uganda in Africa. In the Philippines, both the Roman Catholic Church and the National Council of Churches have encouraged Christian-Muslim dialogue hoping to remove prejudice, recognize common citizenship and develop mutual trust. The Filipino National Council of Churches campaigned successfully for the appointment of a cabinet minister to protect Muslim interests! In the Muslim-majority island of Mindanao, a Roman Catholic bishop has set the whole ministry of his prelature in the context of Muslim-Christian dialogue. Prejudice and distrust remain, but the attempt deserves to be recorded. Ethiopia had given refuge to the first Muslim refugees fleeing from Meccan persecution in the days of the Prophet of Islām. Early Muslim historiography views the Ethiopians with respect because of this initial friendly encounter (which resulted in religious discussion as well!).[6] The contemporary situation is less peaceful. There is considerable tension between the Christian majority and the Muslim minority. Some groups of Muslims have begun armed action against the government and are seeking secession from Ethiopia. Under the present government, followers of both religions are under considerable pressure and a situation where historical relations were good has in fact become one of gloom.

2. Where there is a balance between different religions

The obvious historic example is the Lebanon. Again, early promise in this context has turned sour. The will and ability of Christians and Muslims to live together (mirrored in the Lebanese constitution) have been overtaken by events in the Middle East which have shattered Muslim-Christian understanding. Not all Christians are party to the conflict, however, and many ecumenical and confessional attempts have been made to foster reconciliation in the nation.

Nigeria is an important province in the Anglican communion. It seems that Christians in Nigeria, through the Islām in Africa project and by other means, take an interest in their Muslim fellow citizens and some form of outreach and ministry to Muslims is still possible. It would be fascinating to see a theology of dialogue emerge from a context such as Nigeria's. How do Nigerians of different faiths coexist together in one nation? How do Muslims live by their *Sharīʿah* without seeking to impose it on others? What freedom of worship and witness does one faith have in areas where the other is predominant? Answers to such questions would provide much food for thought for Christians and Muslims in other situations.

3. Where Christians are a minority

In India, the incarnational model for inter-faith encounter has taken deep root in the Christian tradition. Christian presence (in the form of *Ashrams*, for example) in other-faith areas has brought tremendous fruits in terms of increased understanding, mutual stimulus and a common agenda for transforming society. Many Christians have spent a great part of their lives living in close proximity with (say) Hindūs. Often Christians have chosen to live with those of other faiths who are economically depressed or socially oppressed as a sign of solidarity with them, and as a way of bringing about meaningful change. They have made a significant impact and the theology of inter-faith encounter which emerges from such contexts is worth hearing.[7]

In Korea, Christianity has a relatively short history (two hundred years or so at most). Yet the Christian enterprise is flourishing. One of the reasons for this is certainly the fact that during the Japanese occupation, Christians steadfastly refused to worship the emperor at Shinto shrines set up by the imperial authorities. Christianity in Korea is thus associated with nationalism, and the affirmation of Christian distinctiveness is also an affirmation of Koreanness![8] In minority situations the challenge of the gospel to aspects of other faiths, to syncretism and to debased forms of Christianity is often to the fore and needs to be taken seriously in reflection on inter-faith encounter.

Recent theological work in the area of inter-faith dialogue raises certain crucial questions:

1. In the attempt to formulate an inclusive theology and find 'room' for other faiths in the plan of salvation, do we do justice to the distinctiveness of other religions? Non-Christian religions are not simply crypto-Christian religions. They have their own distinct origins, doctrines and rituals which need to be respected and studied for what they are.[9] A willingness to enter into dialogue, however, excludes a position which holds to strict autonomy of the different religions to their own histories, faith-systems and ethical emphases.[10] Religions, although distinct, are accountable to each other and are open to scrutiny by all people in terms of values and truths universally recognized as basic to human society. Such a 'mutual reckoning' must form a significant part of inter-religious dialogue.[11]

2. The Church does not have a monopoly over truth, and truth is recognized and promoted far beyond its boundaries. An appeal is sometimes made to the prologue of St. John's Gospel (1:4, 9) or to Justin Martyr to show that all people have access to the truth through the *Logos spermatikos* (scattered or seminal Word), which illuminates human understanding. It is allowed that natural Man has some knowledge of God and spiritual matters (Acts 14:17; 17:22–29; Romans ch. 1–3). But it is also true that people inevitably corrupt such knowledge of the truth which, therefore, cannot save them (Romans ch. 1–3). Neither in St. John or in the Fathers does

the doctrine of *Logos Spermatikos* teach the presence of the Word in other religions. Bishop Rudvin has shown that the context in Justin is the denial of the truth of other religions. Justin uses the Hellenistic philosophers as allies in this area and postulates the work of the *Logos spermatikos* in them as they developed their critique of the religions around them. Clement of Alexandria (another theologian who discussed the presence of God's eternal Word in the world), too does not refer to the Word as present in other religions.[12]

3. Sometimes it is claimed that various dominical and apostolic encounters with those of other faiths give us 'clues' for inter-religious dialogue. The instances most often quoted are Jesus' encounter with the Syro-Phoenician woman (Mk. 7:24–30 and parallels) and with the centurion (Matt. 8:5–13; Lk. 7:1–10; Jn 4:46–53), Peter's encounter with Cornelius (Acts ch. 10–11) and Paul's with the Athenians (Acts 17:16–34). Why have these first two examples been included in the Gospels? The usual answer is that they were included to point to the approaching universal mission of the Church. Although Jesus' earthly ministry was confined largely to the Jewish nation, there were signs that the preaching of the approaching reign of God would not remain confined to the Jews. They were included to show that the dividing wall of hostility between Jew and non-Jew is broken down in Christ. As the Matthean account of the encounter with the centurion puts it;

> 'I tell you, many will come from East and West and sit at table with Abraham, Isaac and Jacob in the Kingdom of heaven' (Mt. 8:11).

or as Paul says:

> 'For through him we both have access in one Spirit to the Father. So then you are no longer strangers and sojourners, but you are fellow-citizens with the saints and members of the household of God' (Eph. 2:18–19).

It is somewhat far-fetched to hold that an inter-faith encounter is being portrayed in these incidents. The evangelists' point simply is that response to the Messiah comes from the most unexpected sources, that men and women despite their pagan background recognized him. Much is made too of the Cornelius story where a non-Jew is called 'devout' and 'god-fearing'.[13] The whole context of the story, however, shows Cornelius not to have been an adherent of another religion but one of a number of 'god-fearers', i.e., Gentiles who, nevertheless, worshipped the god of Israel, observed the Jewish disciplines of prayer, fasting and alms-giving and only stopped short of circumcision and formal conversion.

Paul's encounter with the Athenians seems to be genuine inter-faith encounter (even Rudvin is forced to acknowledge this).[14] Its significance is that Paul makes a positive evaluation of the 'religiousness' of the Athenians and quotes from their sacred Scriptures, the Poets. It is also true, however, that his proclamation makes the 'unknown' 'known', the Mystery is made manifest and the false aspects of the Athenians' religion (such as idolatry) are condemned.

If this is a model for inter-faith dialogue, then unequivocal proclamation must follow positive evaluation—even at the risk of jeopardizing the dialogue. Paul is patient in the face of unbelief and even ridicule; he is sympathetic to the spiritual aspirations of his listeners and aware of their religious tradition. These attitudes in dialogue deserve commendation. Paul is clear in his presentation of the apostolic preaching of the death and resurrection of Jesus Christ, and this, too, deserves commendation and imitation.

Jesus' encounter with the Samaritan woman (Jn. 4) and the parable of the Good Samaritan (Lk. 10:29–38) are not often mentioned in this context. Yet in the former, Jesus is pointing to a knowledge and worship of God which is post-cultic (Jn. 4: 23–24). Surely this has significance for inter-faith dialogue? In the parable of the Good Samaritan the authentically good man (*moraliter bene*) is the one furthest removed from orthodox religion. This is obviously significant in the formulation of our views regarding those of other faith and of no faith.

Elijah's sojourn with the widow of Zarephath (1 Kgs. 17) and Elisha's healing of Naaman the Syrian (2 Kgs. 5) are sometimes cited as instances of inter-faith encounter. The whole thrust of Elijah's ministry is his persistent refusal to compromise with Baalism. The Elisha story is more suggestive, for it ends with the prophet giving Naaman permission to continue to participate in the cult of the god Rimmon. It is to be noted, however, that Naaman asks pardon of Yahweh and his Prophet for continuing in the worship of Rimmon. Elisha recognized the social and cultural difficulties facing Naaman and permitted him to be a secret believer. This still occurs in many cases where those who have come to believe in Christ cannot openly make a declaration because of their social context. The Melchizedek incident (Gen. 14) and the story of Balaam (Num. ch. 22f.) are certainly a recognition in the Old Testament that God not only speaks to those of other faiths but that *he uses them to speak to us*. This is a radical and necessary conclusion from the evidence. Nevertheless, it remains true that Israel's openness to the interpretation of authentic religious experience, within it or outside, in categories drawn from other traditions is never allowed to compromise the insistence on divine unity.

4. In order to find 'room' for other faiths in the plan and providence of God, attempts have been made to reduce or do away with the concept of Salvation History. It is felt that 'Salvation History', by stressing the election of a particular people, 'tribalizes' God and does not permit the emergence of a universalist theology. In Asia it is sometimes said that the other faiths to which Christianity has to relate are 'cosmic' rather than historical and Christianity too must recast its theology in cosmic and ahistorical terms. Against this, the Church of England's Board of Mission and Unity report rightly states that the election of the people of God is to be understood as an election for witness and service, and leaves no room for pride.[15]

This election is so that the people of God may be 'a light to lighten the Gentiles' (Is. 42:6; Lk. 2:32). Biblical universalism, as developed in the Prophets and the New Testament, is the belief that God's salvation is for all men and that the people of God are agents in conveying this good news to all men. They are not the only agents, for God may work directly in men's hearts, and his grace may cause them to respond to him in repentance and faith. The BMU report states that God's work is through Christ, and those who respond to it are responding through Christ and in solidarity with him (whether or not they are conscious of it).[16] Christ is the locus of the reconciliation: from God to man and from man to God. He is the personification of God's initiative of love, and at the same time, he is the Last Adam who in his radical obedience undoes the effects of the sin of disobedience of the First Adam.

Each group which has a language, a culture and a religious tradition has a salvation history. What constitutes such salvation histories can be determined, however, only when there is a normative Salvation History which allows us to discover elements of salvific value in other traditions. These elements of salvific value may then be regarded as *praeparatio evangelica*. It is not necessary for these salvation histories to be entirely congruent with the religious tradition of a people. The salvation history of a people may challenge its religious traditions at important points.

'The scandal of particularity' of the Bible must be reiterated, but at the same time we must acknowledge God's activity among all peoples and nations. The particular Salvation History of Israel, which is brought to a climax (but not to an end) in the Incarnation, Crucifixion and Resurrection of Our Lord Jesus Christ, is a witness to God's desire to restore all men to fellowship with him, and allows us to discern where there are signs of response to this divine initiative among other peoples. In the Church, all men are invited to become part of God's chosen people by Baptism into Christ's death and by regeneration into his risen life. Barth makes the important point that election of all others is a participation in Christ's election. All those who open themselves to the work of the Holy Spirit and who accept God's offer of free pardon are elected in Christ.[17]

5. The rejection of biblical Salvation History as normative for our understanding of the human predicament and the divine initiative is sometimes accompanied by a 'cosmic' or ahistorical view of Christ. The eternal *Logos,* although supremely manifest in Jesus, is not considered exhausted by the Jesus of history. He may, therefore, be revealed in other religious traditions even in ways dissonant with the revelation in Jesus of Nazareth. Neither Scripture nor tradition see the *Logos* as active in this way. Can we assert, after the Incarnation, activity of the *Logos* apart from the figure of Jesus Christ? We confess the divine-human unity as in the Chalcedonian definition: '. . . one and the same Christ, Son, Lord, unique; acknowledged in two natures without confusion, without change, without division, without separation—the difference of the natures being by no means taken away because of the union, but rather the distinctive character of each nature being preserved and (each) combining in one Person and *Hypostasis*—not divided or separated into two Persons, but one and the same Son and only begotten God, Word, Lord Jesus Christ.' Ignatius had said much the same thing centuries earlier, 'There is one Physician, of flesh and of spirit, originate and unoriginate, God in man, true life in death, Son of Mary and Son of God, first passible and then impassible, Jesus Christ our Lord.'[18]

The Word has become flesh, not simply manifested itself in flesh. Jesus Christ is the full, definitive and final revelation of God for us. Other revelations should be judged in the light of the definitive revelation in Christ which takes place in history, though it points to that which is beyond history. The history of the man Jesus is inescapably, finally and irrevocably tied up with the eternal Word and the one cannot be understood without the other.[19]

6. Another result of this desire to 'flee' history is to begin to regard God the Holy Spirit as somehow distanced from sacred history, working as a kind of benign spiritual influence. The BMU report says that the Spirit's works is 'unpredictable, culturally and historically indeterminate'.[20] This is not the Holy Spirit of the Bible, who is associated from the very beginning with the work of Creation, who inspires the prophets, who authenticates the call

and ministry of Jesus, who is poured out on the Church, who witnesses to and glorifies Jesus. The work of the Spirit in the world seems to be 'prophetic', the Spirit convicts this sinful world of its sins, makes it aware of imminent judgement and also (to those who have ears to hear) of salvation (Jn. 16:7–11). It is the Spirit who convicts a sinner of his sin and makes him 'alive to God' (1 Cor. 2: 10f.). In this sense, part of the work of the Spirit is always ahead of and outside the Church. The Spirit is also continually renewing the Church and equipping it for mission. In the words of John Keble:

'It fills the Church of God; it fills
The sinful world around;
Only in stubborn hearts and wills
No place for it is found'.

The Spirit is omnipresent because he is God, he is active in the Church and the world, but a reverent study of Scripture and tradition would show that he is neither unpredictable nor indeterminate. He is faithful, trustworthy and true; he bears definite witness to Jesus Christ the incarnate, crucified and risen *Logos,* and is always faithful to the revelation of the Triune God in Scripture as it has been received, preserved and reflected upon by the community of faith.

The Christian doctrine and practice of the sacraments (particularly the dominical ones of Baptism and Eucharist) raise the question as to how meaningful and profound can be Christian participation in structured inter-faith worship. Baptism is a participation in Christ's death and his resurrection (Col. 2:11–15). This is not participation in some ahistorical fertility cult of dying and rising gods. It is participation in a unique event in history, which has supra-historical reverberations, and which is seen as having eternal consequences for the initiate. From the earliest times Christian initiation has been regarded as exclusive in the sense that one could not receive Christian Baptism and also receive initiation in (say) a mystery cult. This still holds true: one cannot be a Christian and also be a member of another religion. (This is not always so in other religions; one can, for example, be Shinto and Buddhist at the same time.) Participation in the Eucharist is also regarded as participation in the once-for-all sacrifice at Calvary which obtains the benefits of Christ's death for us. It prevents us from joining the sacrificial rituals of other religions (1 Cor. 10:14–22). In the Muslim context, there is the recurrent problem of Christians who want to know whether it is permissible to eat the meat of sacrificial animals at the Muslim feast of *ʿĪd-ul-Aḍḥā*. The answer that is often given (I believe correctly) is that eating such meat should be avoided, for it is dishonouring to the Eucharist. If we believe that an all-sufficient sacrifice has been offered for us, if we believe that in the Eucharist we are privileged to participate in such a sacrifice, if, moreover, we believe that Scripture and tradition discourage us from participating in the Eucharist as well as in other sacrifices, what choice have we left? The sacraments impart an exclusive character to Christian commitment since they are regarded as a corporate, mystical participation in unique events in sacred history.

The development of a theology of inter-faith dialogue must take into account the varying contexts in which encounter in fact takes place between Christians and those of other faith, it must take serious account of the distinctives of other faiths which may, at times, be opposed to cherished Christian beliefs, and it must reflect profoundly on the 'givens' of Scripture and tradition. Authentic contemporary theology can only arise as a result of a creative engagement between the community of faith as it is today and Scripture and tradition. The same community of faith accepts certain norms by which its life is ordered and its thought governed. While allowing freedom to theologians to engage with Scripture and tradition on the one hand and with contemporary issues on the other, the community must safeguard the authority of norms on which its existence depends. It is only under such conditions that genuine inter-faith dialogue can take place between Christians and those of other faith. Such a dialogue would be a source of enrichment for Christians as they expose themselves to other traditions, while providing an opportunity for humble, loving and serving witness.

CHAPTER 13

The *Qur'ān* as a Bridge in Muslim-Christian Understanding?

The word *Qur'ān* refers primarily to each revelation as it came to *Muḥammad*. Later the word was applied to the collection of revelations (*Ayāt*) vouchsafed to the Prophet of Islām. According to Bell, the word *qara* (from which the word *Qur'ān* is derived), belongs to that religious vocabulary which Christianity had introduced into Arabia: *Qara* means to read or solemnly recite sacred texts, while *Qurān* is the equivalent to the Syriac *qeryana* used to denote the 'reading' or Scripture-lesson. The word *qeryana*, then, was ordinarily applied to the Christian lectionary.[1] It is obviously implied that the 'reading' which has been sent down on *Muḥammad* is continuous with the 'readings' which are possessed by the Christians.

Muḥammad, at any rate, initially may have regarded himself as the interpreter of the Judaeo-Christian monotheistic tradition to the inhabitants of Mecca and its suburbs; 'Thus we have revealed an Arabic reading to you, so that you may warn the mother of cities (i.e. Mecca) and its environs' (42:8). In an attempt to 'universalize' this verse many modern Muslim commentators interpret 'environs' to mean the whole world![2] It seems clear, however, that in the beginning, at any rate, *Muḥammad* was trying to bring the message of monotheism only to the Meccan Arabs in a language they could understand. There are no pre-Muslim translations of the Bible into Arabic: the Jews retained rabbinical Hebrew for their religious language,[3] whereas the Christians used Syriac in their liturgies and in religious discourse.[4]

The rise of Islām can then be regarded as partly due to the failure of Judaism and Christianity to make their message relevant to Arab culture. The fact that *Muḥammad* regarded himself as an Arab Prophet did not stop him later on from claiming that his message had universal significance. Was his message not identical with that of the Prophets of old? *Allāh* always revealed the same truths: 'But you will never find any change in *Allāh*'s behaviour, nor will you find any alteration in it' (35:44). Thus, the claims to universalism are already made in the Meccan *Sūrahs*: 'And we have not sent you except as an evangelist and as a Prophet to all men, but most men do not know this'. And again: 'Say, O mankind, I am truly *Allāh*'s messenger to you all'. (7:158 and see also *Sūrah* 4:79. This is a *Medinan Sūrah*). 'Mankind' could equally well be translated 'people,' and could be made to have a more local application. But whatever *Muḥammad* thought of his own particular vocation, it is clear that he regarded Islām as universal and timeless.

It is also clear that previous revelations have been abrogated as a result of the fresh revelation given to *Muḥammad*. The doctrine of *Naskh* is founded upon the following passage in the *Qur'ān*: 'Whatever revelation we abrogate or cause to be forgotten, we bring a better one or a similar one in its place' (2:106). Even revelations given to *Muḥammad* can be replaced by better revelations. The *Ayat Al-Nāsikha* is the *Qur'ānic* verse which abrogates another verse, known as the *Mansūkh* verse.

Islām accepts that followers of older religions did receive genuine revelation from God and yet also insists that all previous revelations have been subsumed in the *Qur'ān*. This is not dissimilar to the doctrine of 'Fulfilment' that was so popular among Christian missionaries in the 1930's. Just as Christianity was seen as the fulfilment of the truth in other religions, so the *Qur'ān* claims to be the completed truth of the pre-Islāmic religions.

The claims of the *Qur'ān* are verified, according to the Muslim point of view, by the paradox that it was revealed to an illiterate Prophet. 'And you were not a reader of any book before it (i.e. the *Qur'ān*), nor did you write one with your right hand!' (29:48). The actual words *An-Nabī Al-Ummī* occur in 7:158. Pickthall translates this as, 'The Prophet who can neither read nor write', though he suggests in a footnote that this could mean one who has not read the Scriptures (i.e. the Jewish-Christian Bible).[5] *Ẓafarullah Khān*, the *Aḥmadiyya* translator, prefers to translate the phrase as, 'the immaculate Prophet' with the idea that *Muḥammad*, not having read the Jewish-Christian Scriptures, was without pre-conceptions. He was a kind of *tabula rasa* on which God could work.[6] It is part of the *I'jāz*, or miracle of the *Qur'ān*, that it was revealed to such a man. The situation could be compared to one recently reported in *Time* magazine in which an illiterate and non-musical charwoman is alleged to have had an encounter with certain deceased musical composers who are supposed to have dictated musical scores to her. The scores were said to be of high quality! *Muḥammad's* faculties, according to the Muslim view, were not active in the mediation of the revelation except in a purely 'mechanical' way.

Although the *Qur'ān* claims to be a final revelation, it admits that previous Prophets (particularly Jesus and Moses) also had revelations. For example, it says about Jesus: 'And we gave him the Gospel in which is guidance and light' (5:49). *Muḥammad* had probably not seen the New Testament, though he believed it to be in existence and believed it to be uncorrupted. This is illustrated by the following verse: 'Let the people of Gospel judge according to that which *Allāh* has revealed therein, and whoever judges not by that which *Allāh* has revealed is of the rebellious.' (5:50)

Would *Muḥammad* have issued such an invitation if he had known what the Gospel actually contained? The above verse has often been used in Muslim-Christian discussion. The only Christian Gospel accepted by all Christians and certainly in existence at the time of *Muḥammad* was the New Testament as it is known today.[7]

The *Qur'ān* not only admits that the Gospel was vouchsafed to Jesus but also that his disciples were inspired; 'And when we revealed to the disciples how they might believe in me and in my sent one, and they said, we believe and you bear witness that we are Muslims' (5:114). The disciples had some part in passing on the Gospel of Jesus Christ. Perhaps this verse can be used to meet Muslim objections to the authorship of the New Testament. Jesus received the Gospel, but it was the disciples who wrote it down and preserved it.

Even after the *Hijra* (or flight to Mecca), *Muḥammad* continued to believe that the true God was worshipped in Judaism and in Christianity: 'If *Allāh* did not repel the aggression of some people by means of others, cloisters and churches and places of prayer and mosques where the name of *Allāh* is remembered often would most surely be destroyed' (22:40). According to Bell, the incident in *Muḥammad's* mind was the repulsion of the Persians by the Romans. Just as Christians had to fight to retain their places of worship, so the Muslims too must fight the pagan Arabs for the preservation of their holy places.[8]

Muḥammad believed that it was possible for Jews and Christians to obtain salvation, provided they were sincere in their beliefs. 'Lo! those who believe (i.e. Muslims), and those who are Jews and Christians and Sabeans (southern Christians), whoever believes in

Allāh and does right, surely their reward is with their Lord and no fear shall come upon them neither shall they grieve' (2:62).

Keeping all this in mind, does the *Qur'ān* provide a bridge for Christian-Muslim understanding and dialogue? The *Qur'ān's* acceptance that Christians worship the same God as Muslims is favourable to the climate of dialogue. Similarly the *Qur'ānic* acceptance that Christians may find salvation in their own faith is a sign of tolerance. Can we get any further? Islāmic tradition has great reverence for *Muḥammad* (and by implication, other Prophets) as recipients of the *Tanzīl* which has communicated God's will to men on earth.

The Prophets were aided by the Holy Spirit, as the *Qur'ān* puts it, and were mediators of God's Word here on earth.[9] In Christian tradition, however, Jesus (called the Christ) is the eternal word of God become man. In Judaism, it was customary to attribute the speaking of God to a personified Word of God embodying the emanation of speech from the Deity.[10] This Word shares the eternal being of God (what God was, the Word was). It is the Incarnation of this Word from the heart of God that is the basis of the Christian Gospel. Christian and Muslim then share the idea that God sends . . . but differ in whom he sends.

The *Qur'ān* is full of terminology which is common with Christian usage. This could be used as an aid to dialogue. For example, the word *Furqān* is derived from the Syriac *purqana*, meaning salvation. Muslims also associate the meanings of revelation and proof with this word. The use of the word in the *Qur'ān* and its Christian antecedents could be used as a point of departure for a discussion on salvation. There is also a version of the institution of the Eucharist in the *Qur'ān* (5:115f.). The account is somewhat unclear, but the idea that it is a gift from God survives. A Christian teacher can use this verse as a point of departure in explaining the sacrament of Holy Communion to a catechumen (similarly, Baptism is mentioned in 2:138).

The human demand to 'see' God is present in the *Qur'ān* in the story of Moses; 'He (Moses) said, "Lord, show yourself to me that I may behold you." ' God's answer here is in the negative: 'You shall not see me' (7:143). However, in *Sūrah* 20 God does show himself to Moses in the burning bush: 'When he (Moses) came to it (the fire), he heard a call, "Moses, I am truly your Lord, cast off your shoes for you are in the sacred valley of *Ṭuwā*" ' (20:12). If God can show himself to Moses in the burning bush, can he not show himself to us in the man Jesus? Fr. Basetti-Sani has developed a way of reading the *Qur'ān* with Christian eyes. While unqualified approval cannot be given to this method, it has to be acknowledged that the *Qur'ān* is often more open to Christian concerns and meanings that Muslim orthodoxy allows. At the very least, it may be said that a Christian, in reading the *Qur'ān* and in conversation with Muslims, will be alert to implied as well as acknowledged commonalities between Islām and the Christian faith.[11]

The notion of God manifesting himself is present also in *Ṣufism:* 'In every instant he appears in a hundred modes for every day he is upon some labour, if he should reveal himself a hundred thousand times, not one will resemble another.'[12] The desire for God's presence is so strong that it may even lead to idolatry:- 'The desire for the presence of God is the reason for idolatry, Love deceives the soul of the hopeful!'[13] Surely the Gospel can address this strongly felt need?

In a discussion on the *Qur'ān* as a bridge of communication between Christian and Muslim, one cannot escape the insistent Muslim question: Does the Christian accept the *Qur'ān* as genuine? In answering this question, a distinction must be made between revelation and religious experience without any necessary revelational content (as in induced mysticism or as in Nietzsche's 'inspiration' in composing *Thus Spake Zarathustra*). In this sense, the religious experience recorded in the *Qur'ān* is certainly valid, since the only criterion for its validity is its existence and it certainly exists. One can go further and say that in at least some parts of the *Qur'ān* (say the *Fātiḥah* or *ʿAlaq*), there seems to be a genuine encounter with the Supreme Reality of the Universe. Does this amount to a revelation? Yes, in the sense that a revelation is vouchsafed to human beings in creation and in conscience (a fact that the *Qur'ān* makes much of), and this can cause one to ponder upon one's relation to the ultimate meaning of the universe. We can also accept as true all that the *Qur'ān* records accurately of biblical persons and events.

It is difficult to penetrate into the psyche of a subject of religious experience and to distinguish clearly between 'subjective' and 'objective' aspects of religious experience, but surely we can accept the 'religious interrogative' of the *Qur'ān* as a heart-cry and as genuine? We can accept that the *Qur'ān* contains profound reflection on God's revelation of himself in nature and in conscience; we can accept that the *Qur'ān* contains an accurate record of some biblical events; but we cannot accept it as the norm or standard by which all revelation is to be judged. In fact what enables us to judge aspects of the *Qur'ān* as authentic is the normative revelation of the Bible; a record of God's saving acts in the history of a particular people and of their response to God. This cumulative record of God's dealings with his people provides us with criteria for discerning God's activity among other people in other cultures and at different times.

CHAPTER 14

A Christian Assessment of the Cult of Prophet-Veneration

Many Muslims and Christians agree that Muslims should not be called *Muḥammadans* (to do so is considered a survival of the unenlightened past of the West, although several leading Muslims, including *Iqbāl*,[1] apply the word to themselves). Similarly, it is usually agreed Jesus must not be compared with *Muḥammad* but with the *Qur'ān*, the eternal Word of God. *Muḥammad* in Islām is seen merely as a Prophet whose work was simply to bring the Word of God as he understood it to the Arabs of the *Jāhiliyya* (or times of ignorance). This paper raises certain questions about these assumptions by discussing veneration of *Muḥammad* in Islām.

The extent of this veneration in modern Pākistāni society is astonishing. The society nominally adheres to *Sunnī* orthodoxy. But *Muḥammad*-veneration is projected through the mass media, school books and cultural events all of which contribute to the deification of the Arabian Prophet. The following examples illustrate this point:

> 'Though my link with the Divinity of God be severed
> May my hand never let go of the hem of the Chosen One (i.e. *Muḥammad*).'

This is a quotation from a poem by *Maulānā Ẓafar 'Alī Khān*, now being taught in schools. Relationship with the transcendent God is seen to be distant, it is only through *Muḥammad* that one even dares to approach the throne of God. In *Qawwālīs* (a popular cultural event), *Muḥammad* is praised in verse (*Na'at*). This often takes the form of deification:

'If *Muḥammad* had not been, God himself would not have existed!'

This is an allusion to the close relationship *Muḥammad* is supposed to have with God. In the media, *Muḥammad* is often given titles like *Masīḥ uz Zamān* ('Saviour of the World') and *Sarwar-i-Ka'ināt* ('Lord of the Universe'). Are these titles *Muḥammad* would have claimed for himself?

In addition, *Muḥammad's* divinity is explicitly shown in the succession of the *Aḥādīth*, which are popular in *Ṣūfī* circles. For example: The Prophet was sitting one day on a raised platform tying his turban round his head. A believer came to him and asked him to reveal to him (the believer) the nature of Ultimate Reality. At first the Prophet tried to put him off. But on his insistence he agreed to show him his heart's desire. The Prophet and the enquirer then travelled through the seven heavens until they reached a curtain of light. The Prophet told him that this was the furthest they could come. They could not approach Ultimate Reality any closer. The enquirer, however, insisted on seeing behind the curtain. *Muḥammad* tried to dissuade him. But on his insistence he split the curtain into two and revealed the reality behind the curtain: it was *Muḥammad* sitting on a platform tying his turban round his head!

This tradition has affinities with a certain type of *Ṣūfī* literature, e.g. *Farihuddin* ʿ*Aṭṭār's, Manṭiq Uṭ-Ṭair* or *'Conference of Birds'*. Thirty birds travel across the heavens to find Ultimate Reality. When they reach it they discover that it is nothing but the thirty birds themselves! The difference between the tradition and the other stories is that in the stories the aim is generally to propagate monism. In the tradition, the aim is to show the divine nature of *Muḥammad*.

Even *Iqbāl*, custodian of Muslim orthodoxy, uses extraordinarily extravagant language about the Prophet: 'His (i.e. *Muḥammad's*) glory quickened the ardour of the holy ones. At a time when Adam was yet water and clay (i.e. unformed).'[2] This is an allusion to the tradition: 'I was a Prophet while Adam was between water and clay'. The reference is to the doctrine of the *Ḥaqīqat Al-Muḥammadiyya*, or the Pre-existence of the Prophet. In Muslim circles influenced by Neo-Platonism, *Muḥammad* was often regarded as the first emanation from the One: a sort of created *Logos* (comparable to the Arian Christ) from whom the rest of creation proceeds. In another verse, *Iqbāl* seems to go even further:

' "Except God" is the sword, and its edge is "His Servant" (i.e. *Muḥammad*),
If you want it clearer, say, "He is servant".

His servant is the how and wherefore of the universe,
His servant is the inner secret of the universe's being.'[3]

The context makes it clear that the reference is to *Muḥammad*. The justification for this bold doctrine is given by referring to *Qur'ān* 8:17: 'It was not you who threw when you threw but it was God who threw'. This alludes to the Battle of Badr (624 AD) when a handful of Muslims are supposed to have defeated a large Meccan army. The verse originally spoke of divine help given to the whole army, but in time came to be interpreted as divine presence in the Prophet himself.

The Person of *Muḥammad*

The practice of *Muḥammad*-veneration is accompanied by a high doctrine of the person of *Muḥammad*. It is difficult to pin-point the precise origins of the doctrine. Muslims themselves see the germ of it in the *Qur'ān*, particularly in the so-called 'Light Verse' (24:35). Here *Allāh* is regarded as the light and *Muḥammad* as the lamp which contains the light.[4] The *taṣliya* or the close connection between the two articles of the *shahāda* (the Muslim creed): *'Lā ilah ilā Allāh'* (there is no god but *Allāh*), and *'Muḥammad Ar-Rasūl Allāh'* (*Muḥammad* is the apostle of *Allāh*) is often taken to indicate *Muḥammad's* close connection with the Divine Unity. The doctrine developed under Neo-Platonic and Christian inspiration. Neo-Platonism posed its ancient problem for the Muslim mind: How did the many proceed from the One? Christianity supplied a possible answer by postulating a duality (and therefore a principle of differentiation), in the Divine Unity in its doctrine of the *Logos*. The *Logos*, or the Divine Idea, is the locus of the differentiation which proceeds from the Unity.

Aḥmad and *Fadl*, disciples of *Nazzām*, a *Muʿtazilī* theologian (c. 830 AD), accepted that the earthly revelation of the *Logos* was Jesus Christ.[5] The whole doctrine was, however, soon transferred to the person of the Prophet. The essence of the last of the Prophets is said to have been created first in the form of a dense and luminous point, all other souls are supposed to have emanated from this *Nūr Muḥammadī*. Another variant of the doctrine is the *Ḥaqīqat Al-Muḥammadiyya*. A distinction is made between God's *Ḥaqq* (or Ultimate Truth) which pertains to his *Dhat* (or essence) and his *Haqā'iq* (or truths) which pertain to his *Ṣifāt* (or qualities). The *Ḥaqā'iq* of *Allāh* are individualizations of His essence, and describe His relationship to the world. The *Ḥaqīqat Al-Muḥammadiyya* is the Divine Essence in its first individualization (i.e. in the person of the pre-existent *Muḥammad*). The doctrine was first developed by *Ibn ʿArabī* (d. 1240 AD), but became formative for later Islāmic mysticism.

Orthodoxy upholds the primacy of the eternal *Qur'ān*, but the masses have often been devoted to the created *Logos*, i.e. to *Muḥammad*. He is thought to be instrumental in the act of creation and all creation is thought to have been created for him. This is illustrated in an old *Ḥadith* (or traditional saying): 'If it had not been for you, I would not have created the heavens.' Among the *Shīʿa*, the doctrine is not limited to the historical *Muḥammad*. It is often developed in either of two ways: first, the 'prophetic light' may be seen as transmitted from one age to another by means of a spirit which manifests itself in some individual. Second, the light may be seen as transmitted in a spermatic germ from male to male. In either case, the doctrine of *Khatm Al-Nubuwwat* (the Finality of *Muḥammad's* Prophethood) is challenged. The light appearing in the historical *Muḥammad* continues to appear through the ages in other 'elect' figures as well.

The practice of invoking a blessing on the Prophet and upon his family and friends is an ancient and universal Muslim custom. It comes immediately after the *Ṣalāt*, or mandatory prayer. The practice is known as *Darūd*, and must be the most popular part of Muslim devotion. Considerable devotional literature has, therefore, grown up around the subject. One of the most popular devotional manuals is *Dalā'il Al-Khairāt* (*Guides to the Good* by *Al-Jazūlī*).[6] This book contains a list of the 201 names of *Muḥammad*, (as against ninety-nine for God!) Many of the names are identical to certain divine names, except that in the case of *Muḥammad* they are without the definite article. Moreover, the *Asmā Al Ḥusna* (names of God), are given just before the *Asmā An-Nabī* (names of the Prophet), almost to encourage comparison!

Two scholars, Dr. R. Y. Ebeid and Dr. M. J. L. Young, recently called attention to Leeds Arabic MS 12, which is a list of *Muḥammad's* 201 names. They claim such lists are rare in Islāmic literature and that this is because they invite comparison with the Divine Names.[7] Bishop Rudvin has effectively refuted these claims. The lists, as we have seen, are easily available and comparison is often made with the divine names.

Let us compare some of the names in the *Asmā Al-Ḥusna* and in the *Asmā An-Nabī*:

1. *'Azīzun* with *Al-ʿAzīzu* (beloved and the Beloved).
2. *Raḥīmun* with *Ar-Raḥīmu* (merciful and the Merciful).
3. *Jabbārun* with *Al-Jabbāru* (mighty and the Mighty One).
4. *Karīmun* with *Al-Karīmu* (benevolent and the Benevolent One).
5. *Ḥaqqun* with *Al-Ḥaqqu* (truth and the Truth).

6. *Qawīun* with *Al-Qawīu* (strong and the Strong One).
7. *Barrun* with *Al-Barru* (righteous and the Righteous One).
8. *ʿAfūun* with *Al-ʿAfūu* (forgiver and the Forgiver).
9. *Nūrun* with *An-Nūru* (light and the Light, this is an important identification as *Nūr* is often identified with God's absoluteness).

It is clear that many of God's titles are also used of the Prophet, although they appear in a somewhat reduced sense.

Reciters of *Darūd* are promised heavenly wives, heavenly palaces, indulgence for sins and general felicity both in this life and in the next. An interesting letter appeared in a local paper recently. The writer commented on the laxity in invoking a blessing on the Prophet whenever his name is mentioned in modern literature. The words, 'Peace be upon him' or even the initials P.B.U.H. are often used. The writer points out that the correct form is: '*Ṣalla'l Lāho Wassalām ʿAleihi*' (the blessing and the peace of God be upon him). He quotes a *Ḥadith* to the effect that reserve in the matters of *Darūd* is the worst form of disobedience! He also refers to a conversation between *Muḥammad* and one of the *Ṣaḥāba* (close companions of the Prophet) *Ḥadrat Kaʿab*. *Kaʿab* asks *Muḥammad* how much of his *Duʿā* (i.e. personal prayer as opposed to *Ṣalāt*), he should reserve for reciting *Darūd*. Would a quarter be enough? *Muḥammad* says yes, but if he recites more it would be beneficial. This goes on until the *Saḥābī* says that he is going to reserve the entire *Duʿā* for reciting *Darūd* (i.e. he is not going to make any prayer requests for himself). *Muḥammad* then says that if *Kaʿab* does this, all his needs will be met and that he will lack nothing.[8] A typical *Darūd* goes something like this:

> 'God's blessing and great peace be upon our Lord *Muḥammad* and upon his family and upon his companions.'

Dalā'il Al-Khairāt is used in *Dhikr* (recitation designed to induce a mystical state) and in *Ṣūfī* circles. Its use to obtain material favours is also widespread. It is often published alongside the *Qaṣīda Burda* (a poem in praise of the Prophet by *Al-Buṣairī*) and other devotional works. The Leeds manuscript (dated 1851 AD) is almost certainly a copy from *Dalā'il Al-Khairāt*. We can say this because of *Dalā'il Al-Khairāt's* popularity and antiquity. Bishop Rudvin comments that the agreement between the two lists is so close that either one is a copy from the other or both writers had access to the same source. The latter seems unlikely and one has to opt for dependence.[9]

What effect should an awareness of the cult of *Muḥammad* veneration have upon the Christian approach to the Muslim? First, we should be cautious about using *Qur'ānic* titles of Jesus as 'proofs' of his divinity, as *Muḥammad* is also given extravagant titles. In addition to sharing certain names with *Allāh* himself, he also has some names which in Christian circles would be considered Christological or pneumatological. For example:

1. *Munjin* or *Munajjī*, both having the sense of saviourhood.
2. *Ṣirāṭ Allāh* and *Ṣiraṭ Al Mustaqīm* (the way of God and the right way or true way).
3. *Wakīl* (intercessor or mediator and advocate). This title is important, because Muslims consider the counsellor promised in John's Gospel to be *Muḥammad*. Surprisingly enough, pneumatological titles like *Rūḥ Al-Quds* and *Rūḥ Al-Ḥaqq* (Holy Spirit and Spirit of Truth) are also used of *Muḥammad* in *Dalā'il Al-Khairāt*.

Is the *Qur'ānic* Jesus in any way unique? The *Qur'ānic* view of *Muḥammad* is very probably 'lower' than the view of later devotees. If the person of Jesus as understood in the *Qur'ān* is compared with the *Qur'ānic* view of other Prophets, certain titles used of Jesus make it possible to hold that the *Qur'ānic* view of Jesus is higher than the *Qur'ān*ic view of other Prophets. The title *Kalimatullāh* (Word of God) is not used of *Muḥammad* in *Dala'il Al-Khairāt* (although Bishop Rudvin claims that it is used of *Muḥammad* in other lists). *Kalimatohu* is of course used of Jesus Christ in 4:171, and it is never used of *Muḥammad* in the *Qur'ān*. Jesus' virgin birth also makes him unique as 'a Word' from *Allāh*, (4:171; 19:34f.). There are other indications that the *Qur'ān* considers Jesus exceptional. The *Qur'ānic* reluctance to admit that the Jews could have slain Jesus (4:157) is one example. This reluctance is strange if Jesus were a 'mere' Prophet, as the standard *Qur'ānic* charge against the Jews is precisely that they slew the Prophets! (2:61, 91) *Muḥammad's* own death is discussed as well (3:144). Muslim apologists sometimes claim that Jesus couldn't have been slain as he was not only a Prophet (*Nabī*), but also an Apostle (*Rasūl*). *Muḥammad,* however, is also *Rasūl*, and the possibility of his being slain is clearly present in the *Qur'ān*. Is there docetism in the background here: Jesus did not die, he could not die since he only appeared to be a man and was not so truly. Such a view would then place Jesus in a very special position indeed!

Post-*Qur'ānic* Literature

In the post-*Qur'ānic* literature, extravagant titles are used of *Muḥammad* without reserve. While some are due to the ardour of devotion, others may be the result of Christian influence. Such titles appear to identify *Muḥammad* with God, and sound Christological or pneumatological to Christian ears. Certain parables of Jesus are put in *Muḥammad's* mouth by the traditionists. Other New Testament passages are also attributed to the Prophet (e.g. 1 Cor. 2:9).

Incarnational language is also used about *Muḥammad*. Some *Sunnīs* consider the *Nūr Al-Muḥammadiyya* to be incarnate in the historical *Muḥammad*. Among the *Shīʿa*, the prophetic light is regarded either as a spirit incarnate in a different individual in every age, or as a germ which is transferred from one generation to another.

Muḥammad **as Intercessor**

Muḥammad's intercessory role is another aspect of the veneration of the Prophet. The title *Shafīʿun* illustrates this point, as does *Sāḥib Ash-Shifāʿh* (Lord of Intercession), which is used in the *Dalāʾil*. Many stories of how *Muḥammad* will intercede for believers on the last day emphasize this. *Muḥammad's* role as intercessor is based on certain *Qurʾānic* texts (20:109; 34:23; 43:86). The texts do not, however, mention *Muḥammad* by name. The *Muʿtazilites* (the Rationalists) did not believe in *Muḥammad's* intercessory role. They held that such an intercession would be contrary to the justice of God. They quoted *Qurʾān* 2:49, where it is clearly said that there will be no *Shifāʿh* on the last day.[10]

Superstition is closely linked to *Muḥammad's* role as intercessor. For example, by writing certain verses of the *Qaṣīda Burda* on the viscera of a deer and tying it on one's right arm one can learn Arabic more quickly! Certain other verses of the same poem are considered effective for relief from epilepsy if they are written on a strip of blue cloth and the cloth is then burnt and the smoke is inhaled by the sufferer. The chapter on the benefits of *Darūd* in *Dalāʾil* promises a believer (on the strength of a *Ḥadīth*) that if *Muḥammad* is blessed one hundred times on a Friday, eighty years' sins would be forgiven! The Prophet is reported to have said that if one blessed him frequently, he would have many wives in paradise. Similarly, one who recited a thousand blessings on the Prophet is promised many things including a palace (*Qaṣr*) in heaven for each blessing![11] It is well known that *Muḥammad's* name (together with *Allāh*) is used as a charm. Such charms may either be worn on the body, kept in the house, or consumed in a drink or in sweetmeats.

A Christian Response

Awareness of the cult should produce an appropriate and adequate Christian response. *Muḥammad*-veneration implies a rejection of the Muslim view of God. The orthodox so emphasize God's transcendence (*tanzīh*) that they sever any link between God and his world. *Muḥammad* then becomes the locus to which all religious devotion is directed. He is tangible and concrete, as opposed to the abstract Almighty. The phenomenon illustrates the human need to 'touch' and to 'handle' God. Human beings continually waver between their awe of God's holiness and their need for intimacy with the source of their being. The Christian should remember this when explaining the Christian doctrine of the Incarnation.

There is also tension in Muslims regarding the Prophet's person. On the one hand, Muslims would normally agree that *Muḥammad* was but a mortal man (the spirit of 3:144), on the other, their whole cultural conditioning teaches them to regard *Muḥammad* at least as 'nearly divine'. This tension exists both within the individual and in the community.

Set against this tension is the nearly unanimous (allowing for heresies) testimony of the Scriptures and the Church to the divinity of Jesus Christ. This testimony is second only to Jesus' own claims (not only in John but in the Synoptics as well, e.g. Mt. 11:27; Mk. 14:62). Moreover, Jesus' claims were not made in a vacuum. They were made with the background of Old Testament prophecy concerning the Messiah in mind (e.g. Mt. 22:41).

Muḥammad exhorts the Christians to look into the Gospel for guidance (5:50). The only gospels in existence at the time of *Muḥammad* were the New Testament ones, more or less as we know them today, or the 'apocryphal' ones which have an equally 'high' Christology. There is some evidence in the *Qur'ān* to suggest that *Muḥammad* knew of at least some of the apocryphal gospels. Many early versions of the New Testament came from the neighbourhood of Arabia (e.g. the Syriac *Peshitta*, the two Coptic versions, etc.), and *Muḥammad* may have known of their existence. The early Muslim commentators and apologists never refer to an alternative, which might have strengthened their case. The comparatively recent and patently false *'Gospel of Barnabas'*, sometimes used by Muslim apologists today, is not mentioned in the early Islāmic writings. As I have tried to show elsewhere, its antiquity cannot be maintained on critical grounds and its genuineness cannot be maintained on theological grounds (among other things, it differs from the *Qur'ān* on several matters!). It is highly improbable that *Muḥammad* had access to any generally received Christian document which had a 'low' Christology. The only Gospel acceptable to Christians in *Muḥammad's* day would have been the New Testament.[12]

The purity of Jesus' life has always been recognized in Muslim ascetical and mystical circles.[13] Also the moral excellence of his teaching compared to the harsh legalism of certain kinds of Islāmic fundamentalism, is being recognized by many Muslims today. In addition, Muslims have always seen in Jesus the miracle-performing Prophet *par excellence*. Christ's suffering, rather than currently fashionable triumphalism, is often seen by many today as a model for the servants of God.[14]

Part IV
The Christian and Social Order

Introduction

Christians believe in a Just God who requires justice of human beings in their dealings with their fellows. In both the Old and the New Testaments, there is a passionate and prophetic concern for justice; the strong are to be fair in their dealings with the weak, there should be no oppression of the stranger, rulers and ruled alike are subject to the divine law. Justice in the Bible, however, is not simply a legal abstraction. It is the outworking of love and cannot, therefore, exist without other biblical virtues such as mercy and forgiveness. The teaching of Jesus is constantly warning us against the spiritually barren legalism which can result from too much attention to the *letter* of the law and not enough attention to the *spirit* of it. The teaching of our Lord constantly emphasizes the internal at the expense of the merely external, the meaning at the expense of form. A truly just society can never be a merely legalist society. Legalism ultimately results in injustice, for it fails to take note of circumstances and personalities. A truly just society must also be a humane society which is capable of showing mercy and forgiveness while at the same time it upholds the law.

The first two Chapters of the following Part were written at a time when there was a lively debate going on in Pākistān on the enforcement of *Sharīʿah* (or Islāmic Law) in the country. Many Muslims thought that the nation would become a truly just society only if the *Sharīʿah* was enforced in its entirety and rigour. There were others, however, who held that the *Sharīʿah* had been given in particular circumstances, and, while as Muslims they believed in the eternal validity of the principles and values of the *Sharīʿah*, they also realized that the way it was enforced in the 7th century was not necessarily the way it should be implemented today. At this point, the government invited the Christian members of parliament to present the Christian point of view on particular issues, and they in turn asked the present writer to advise them on these matters.

The third Chapter was written for a meeting of theologians concerned to relate the Gospel of 'Jesus Christ: Redeemer and Liberator' to pressing contemporary issues: one of these issues was the political, social and economic repression under which perhaps the majority of the human race lives. In what way can the Gospel's offer of wholeness be related to such a context?

CHAPTER 15

The Church and the Socio-Political Order*

From the very earliest times, polity within Christianity has been what Bishop Alexander Malik has called 'A Theo-democracy'.[1] It has been recognized that ultimate sovereignty belongs to God, but in practice the divine will has been discerned in the wishes of the faithful, confirmed by the world-wide leadership of the Church. 'The *Didache*' or '*Teaching of the Apostles*', a first century document on Church order, puts it in this way: 'Appoint for yourselves therefore bishops and deacons worthy of the Lord, men that are meek and not lovers of money, true and reliable.'[2] Chadwick, commenting on early Church order, observes, 'The actual choice of the candidate (for the office of bishop) rested with the whole congregation, clergy and people together . . . election by the people likewise played a large part in the ordination of presbyters and deacons.'[3] The laying on of hands itself was a recognition and confirmation by the universal leadership of the Church of the choice of the people which in turn was thought of as guided by the Holy Spirit (Acts 6:1–6; 13:3; cf. Num. 8:10).[4]

In the Eastern Church, the canons of the Synod of Seleucia (410 AD) refer to the Consecration and 'perfection' of popularly-elected bishops. In the Church of the East (or the Nestorians), popular election of bishops continued down into Islāmic times. In the ninth century, Timothy, Patriarch of Baghdād, while issuing instructions to the Indian Church regarding the appointment of bishops,

*This paper was written in response to a request for advice from a Christian member of Parliament who was serving on the Parliamentary Constitution Committee.

assumes that these bishops would be the choice of the Indians themselves (though they need not be, and often were not, Indians).[5]

The large Coptic Church of Egypt and Ethiopia continues to this day to practice universal adult franchize in the conduct of its own affairs. A recent handbook states, 'According to the earliest laws and regulations of the Coptic Church, the Pope (that is, the Patriarch), as well as all members of the Holy Orders, are elected by those over whom they will preside. The election of the deacons and priests is naturally restricted to their own parishes, that of the bishops to their own dioceses while the Pope is elected by general vote.'[6]

The polity of the Christian Church itself is democratic, although it is possible for the Church to exist within the context of other systems. The survival and expansion of the Church under both the Roman and Persian Empires is evidence that the Church can survive in 'absolutist' situations. Again, the Church's survival in the Islāmic Empire shows us that the Church was able to survive in a system which was at first a benevolent oligarchy but later became a hereditary monarchy.

Within the Persian and Islāmic Empire, the Church functioned as a *millat* (in this case, the Muslims inherited the Persian system virtually intact). This *millat* was subject to its own ruler (who was also its religious head), whose appointment had to be approved by the state. It could make its own laws (again, subject to state approval) and disobedience to them could be punished by state authority. It could own buildings, endowments and institutions. A person could leave the *millat* by abandoning the religion of the *millat* but while s/he remained in it, s/he was bound to obey its rules.[7]

The Church must, however, commend its own recognition of the theo-democratic principle to the wider society around her. The Church recognizes this principle to be of evangelical origin. It is for this reason that it is applied to her own life and it is for this reason that she can commend it to others. As Jacques Maritain, a modern Roman Catholic scholar, puts it:

> 'Christianity announced to the peoples the Kingdom of God and the life to come, it has taught them the unity of the human race, the natural equality of all men, children of the same God and redeemed by the same Christ, the inalienable dignity of every soul fashioned in the image of God, the dignity of labour and the dignity of the poor, the supremacy of inner values and of good will over external values, the inviolability of consciences, the exact vigilance of God's justice and providence over the great and the small. It has taught them the

obligation imposed on those who govern and on those who have possessions to govern in justice, as ministers of God, and to manage the good entrusted to them to the common advantage, as God's stewards, the submission of all to the law of work and the call to all to share in the freedom of the sons of God.

It has taught them the sanctity of truth and the power of the Spirit, the Communion of the saints, the divine supremacy of redeeming love and mercy, and the law of brotherly love which reaches out to all, even to those who are our enemies, because all men, to whatever social group, race, nation or class they may belong, are members of God's family and adopted brothers of the Son of God. Christianity proclaimed that where love and charity are, there God is, and that it is for us to make every man our neighbour by loving him as ourselves, and by having compassion for him, that is, in a sense, by dying unto ourselves for his sake. Christ cursed the rich and the Pharisees. He promised the poor, and those who suffer persecution for the sake of justice, that they shall inherit the kingdom of heaven, the weak that they shall inherit the earth, those who mourn that they shall be comforted, those that hunger and thirst after justice, that they shall be satisfied, the merciful that they shall obtain mercy, the pure in heart that they shall see God, the peacemakers that they shall be called sons of God. He declared that everything that is done to the meanest of his brothers is done to him, and he gave his disciples a new commandment to love one another as he himself has loved them.'[8]

According to Maritain, the democratic impulse has arisen in human history as a temporal manifestation of the inspiration of the Gospel, and it conforms with other aspects of the Christian message.

One element of Christian tradition of which we must take note is the separation of the sacred and the secular. This is based, of course, on dominical teaching, 'Render to Caesar the things that are Caesar's and to God the things that are God's' (Mark 12:17 and parallels). This does not mean, of course, that our faith has nothing to say to the secular world, nor does it mean that there may be areas of a Christian's life which remain unaffected by the Gospel. It is quite clear that Christ's teaching encompasses the whole of human life. A person's relationship to his God, to his family, to his neighbour, to his enemy, his devotional life, his alms-giving, his attitude to the poor and the oppressed, his relationship to the state and to those in secular authority. All these are areas directly governed by evangelical teaching. The distinction between sacred and secular is meant to free the Church from temporal enslavement and to ensure that the state does not become a tyranny with sacred pretensions. It is basic to the idea of a free and plural society. Inevitably, a state or a ruler with sacred pretensions becomes intolerant of religious minorities which do not subscribe to the ideology which underpins the system. Also, a state or a rule with sacred pretentions is on the way to becoming absolutist; to disobey it is supposed to be disobedience to God. An ideological state is particularly prone to the dangers of totalitarianism in the sense that it seeks more and more to govern every aspect of a citizen's life.[9] We may allow, for example, that Islām should govern the totality of a Muslim's life (this indeed is true of Christianity and the Christian as well), but may an Islāmic state govern the totality of a citizen's life (whether he is a Muslim or not)?[10]

There are lessons to be learnt from history. The Christian minority in Pākistān does not wish to become a disenfranchized, segregated group which has little or nothing to contribute to national life. This has happened in the past and we need to ensure that it does not happen again. Nor would we like certain restrictive practices to be restored. We would continue to wish to be treated as equal citizens with freedom of worship and proclamation; free to build, maintain and manage our own institutions. In particular, any move to reinforce the so-called 'Ordinance of *ʿUmar*' is to be resisted.[11]

Not only are there lessons to be learnt from the past, but reassurances to be sought for fears which have arisen in the present. There are groups in the country campaigning for the curtailment of minority rights and these need to be checked.

What of the future? We would hope that in any future polity, our country would acknowledge the ultimate sovereignty of God which is exercized through the people. Mr. Massey observes, quite rightly, that this is reflected in the history of constitution-making in Pākistān and especially in the preamble to the 1973 Constitution.[12] Granted that the polity of Pākistān will be in accordance with Islāmic ideals and aspirations, the basis of such a polity should then be the *Qur'ānic* conception of human beings as the vice-regents of God fulfilling the trust which they have undertaken.[13] Only in such a broad and liberal system would the minorities feel at home. It is certainly true that our problems and opportunities are peculiar to us, but this is true of every country. We must devise a durable polity in accordance with our needs. It is difficult, however, to agree with the view that we cannot benefit from the constitutions or systems of other nations.[14] Pākistān is neither a geographical nor a political island. We are, necessarily, affected by events outside Pākistān. Moreover, there are countries with problems and opportunities which are similar to ours. May we not benefit from their experience and experiment? Which nomenclature we use for our polity is of secondary importance. What is important is to safeguard the principle of popular, representative government and the franchize of all sections of the population. We must beware of serving only our own community interest. We must work for the good of the entire nation and especially of the poor, the weak and the oppressed.

CHAPTER 16

Retaliation: A Response*

The Jewish View

The *lex talïonis* (law of retaliation) as a legal principle was reasonably common in the ancient Middle East. It was to be found, for example, in the Code of *Hammurabi*, as well as in the Hittite Laws.[1] The occurrence of *lex talionis* in the Old Testament is, therefore, to be understood within this general Middle Eastern context.[2] In the Pentateuch the *lex talionis* is mentioned three times:

1. 'If any harm follows, then you shall give life for life, eye for eye, tooth for tooth, hand for hand, foot for foot, burn for burn, wound for wound, stripe for stripe' (Exodus 21:23, 24).
2. 'When a man causes a disfigurement in his neighbour, as he has done it shall be done to him, fracture for fracture, eye for eye, tooth for tooth; as he has disfigured a man, he shall be disfigured' (Lev. 24:19, 20).
3. 'Your eye shall not pity; it shall be life for life, eye for eye, tooth for tooth, hand for hand, foot for foot' (Dt. 19:21).

In addition, there is the punishment in Dt. 25:11, 12 which, though not strictly according to the principles of *lex talionis*, is, nevertheless, retaliatory. It is known that the crime of murder was always punished with death and that no compensation was permitted in such a case (Num. 35:16ff.). In other cases the law lost some of its cutting edge: the section in Exodus, for instance, which

*Advice given to Christian Members of Parliament at their request at the time the proposed law on retaliation was being debated.

prescribes *lex talionis* also provides for its limitation and for compensation in cases that *prima facie* appear to come under *lex talionis* (Ex. 21:18, 22, 26–27). As one Roman Catholic scholar puts it, 'this formula seems to have lost its force, merely asserting the principle of proportionate compensation'.[3] We are told that, 'this law was never, at least in any even semi-civilized society, carried out literally. The Jewish jurists argued rightly that to carry it out literally might in fact be the reverse of justice, because it might involve the displacement of a good eye or a good tooth for a bad eye or a bad tooth. And very soon the injury done was assessed at money value.'[4] Compensation was assessed, keeping the following five factors in mind:

1. The nature and extent of the injury.
2. The pain caused.
3. Cost of treatment.
4. Loss of time.
5. Indignity suffered.

The biblical *lex talionis* was, then, a limitation on endless blood-feuding. It was restricted in scope, it was juridicially determined and, in most cases, literal application was replaced by a system of appropriate compensation.

The Islāmic View

Islāmic law on retaliation (*Qiṣāṣ*) and compensation (*Diya*) appears to be based on two passages in the *Qur'ān*. First, with respect to homicide: 'O ye who believe! The law of retaliation is prescribed for you in cases of murder: the free for the free, the slave for the slave, the woman for the woman. But if any remission is made by the brother of the slain, then grant any reasonable demand and compensate him with handsome gratitude. This is a concession and a mercy from your Lord. After this whoever exceeds the limits shall be in grave penalty' (2:178). In striking contrast to Jewish law, homicide is deemed a compoundable offence here. The second passage is more general: 'We ordained therein for them; Life for life, eye for eye, nose for nose, ear for ear, tooth for tooth and wounds equal for equal. But if anyone remits the retaliation by way of charity, it is an act of atonement for himself. And if any fail to judge by what God has revealed they are wrong-doers' (5:48).

One of the first points of comparison with Mosaic Law is the relative absence of the juridicial element in the Islāmic Law of *Qiṣāṣ* as stated in the *Qur'ān*. 'Homicide remains an offence which falls into the category of civil injuries rather than that of public offences or crimes.'[5] It is for this reason that all offences which come under *Qiṣāṣ* are regarded as compoundable. The *Hedaya,* a compendium of law for Muslims, which has been in use for over two hundred years in the sub-continent, tells us that retaliation in cases other than homicide was not generally inflicted but that an appropriate fine (or compensation), in strict proportion to the injury, was imposed.[6] *Ḥanifite* Law (but not *Shāfi-ite*) prescribes equality for non-Muslims in matters of retaliation and compensation. This is also allowed by *Maudūdī.*[7] Any modern version of the law is expected to provide equality in this matter for non-Muslims.

A Christian View

John Bligh, in his book on the Sermon on the Mount, makes the point that the 'antitheses' of Matthew 5:21–45 should be understood in terms of the fulfilment saying of the preceding verse 17. In other words, the antitheses are not antitheses at all, but radically new ways of understanding the theses. So murder is not just literal killing, but also the intention to harm; adultery is not just the physical act, but evil desire as well and so on. Now, in this context, what does the saying on retaliation mean?

> 'You have heard that it was said, "An eye for an eye and a tooth for a tooth." But I say to you, "Do not resist one who is evil. But if any one strikes you on the right cheek, turn to him the other also; and if any one would sue you and take your coat, let him have your cloak as well; and if any one forces you to go one mile, go with him two miles. Give to him who would borrow from you." '

> 'You have heard that it was said, "You shall love your neighbour and hate your enemy." But I say to you, "Love your enemies and pray for those who persecute you so that you may be sons of your Father who is in heaven. For he makes his sun rise on the evil and on the good, and sends rain on the just and on the unjust." '

Jesus does not abrogate the Law on retaliation, says Bligh, but rather suggests a new way of understanding it. The principle of retaliation was to repay evil for evil. Jesus is suggesting that it should be: repay evil with good! Retaliate by doing good to someone who has harmed you.[8] This new way of understanding retaliation is not wholly new, nor is it totally alien to the Judaic tradition. The 'newness' of Jesus' teaching here, as elsewhere, consists in bringing out the implications of traditional biblical teaching which has been neglected.

Leviticus 19:18, for example, teaches: 'You shall not take vengeance or bear any grudge against the sons of your own people, but you shall love your neighbour as yourself: I am the Lord.' Kidner, commenting on this verse, says, 'This "great commandment" envisages a provocative situation, not a naturally harmonious one, in which to carry out its demand. And if it seems unduly parochial with its mention of "your own people", it is to make sure that at least at home, if nowhere else, you should learn to live at peace. But if charity has begun at home, verse 34 forbids it to end there. "The stranger . . . shall be to you as the native, and you shall love him as yourself." '[9] Proverbs 25:21–22 similarly prescribes the way one is to treat one's enemy: 'If your enemy is hungry, give him bread to eat; and if he is thirsty, give him water to drink.' For the Christian, then, retaliation in the sense of returning evil for evil is absolutely forbidden at the individual level. Also, more positively, the Christian is enjoined to return good for evil. Vengeance, even when limited by law, tends to brutalize society, and cannot be the basis for civilized social relations. This teaching is directed towards the individual who suffers. As far as the offender is concerned, the Gospels teach the principle of restitution. This is admirably illustrated in the story of Zacchaeus the dishonest tax-collector who repented. As a sign of his repentance he says, 'Behold, Lord, the half of my goods I give to the poor; and if I have defrauded anyone of anything, I restore it four-fold.'[10] Another example may be found in confession rites in the Roman Catholic, Orthodox and Anglican traditions where absolution is not given until at least a willingness to make restitution is discerned in the penitent. Restoration of a penitent to Christian fellowship and worship can take place only when he is willing to make appropriate restitution (Matt. 5:23–24).

The New Testament has clear teaching about the role of the state in the punishment of offenders (Romans 13:1–7; 1 Peter 2:13–17). Christians must, however, if they are to continue to be faithful to Christ's teaching, press for the principle of forgiveness to be built into our society's theory and practice of punishment. Society cannot, of course, simply overlook every wrong done to it or to its members. This would be a licence for lawlessness. Unfortunately, in our fallen world there must be punishment. How then can punishment itself include forgiveness? An adequate Christian view of punishment must include the following factors:

1. *Retribution:* The punishment must fit the crime. As Kidner says, '. . . retribution, properly understood, is the only sound basis of punishment, since it alone asks the question "what does this man deserve for what he did?" '[11] Deterrence is an effect produced by punishment, but it must not become the only criterion for punishment. If it does, punishment tends to become

disproportionate to the crime. In the words of C. S. Lewis, 'There is no sense in talking about a "just deterrent or a just cure." ' We demand of a deterrent not whether it is just but whether it will deter. We demand of a cure not whether it is just, but whether it succeeds. When we cease to consider what the criminal deserves and consider only what will cure him or deter others, we have tacitly removed him from the sphere of justice altogether: instead of a person, a subject of rights, we now have a mere object, a patient, a 'case'. 'It will be in vain for the rest of us, speaking simply as men, to say "but this punishment is hideously unjust, hideously disproportionate to the criminal's deserts." The experts with perfect logic will reply, "but nobody was talking about deserts. No one was talking about punishment in your archaic vindictive sense of the word. Here are the statistics proving that this treatment deters . . . that this other treatment cures. What is your trouble?" '[12]

2. *Reformation:* The punishment must give the criminal an opportunity for reform. There is no necessary contradiction in holding to both a retributive and reformatory view of punishment: The principle of retribution gives us some idea of what the criminal deserves. The form of the punishment, may, however, be guided by reformatory considerations.[13]

3. *Rehabilitation:* The punishment must not make this vital task more difficult. The criminal should be prepared to take his/her place once again as a useful and productive member of society. Punishments, therefore, which mutilate the body or damage the mind should not have the endorsement of Christians. The death penalty should also be opposed for the above reasons and also for the ghastly possibility of executing the wrong person.

The Christian is not arguing for a 'holiday' for criminals. The retributive aspect of punishment should ensure a certain amount of suffering and deprivation. The other two aspects, however, should ensure that this suffering has a certain 'redemptive' value too (at least potentially), both for the criminal and for society.

At the individual level then, the Christian is not only forbidden to retaliate with evil for evil but is commanded to return good for evil. Church and State, in their different ways, should compel the offender to make appropriate restitution. The State and, in some cases, the Church, should punish the offender according to his deserts. At the same time, it should be ensured that the possibilities of reformation and rehabilitation are built into the system of punishment.

CHAPTER 17

Wholeness and Fragmentation: The Gospel and Repression

The biblical view of creation speaks of humankind as having been created in the image of God and as having been given the role of steward over the rest of creation.[1] This implies that human beings have a certain dignity and freedom *vis à vis* the rest of creation. The idea that human beings are free, responsible beings is characteristic of the Judaeo-Christian tradition. Islām too, standing within this broad tradition, affirms humankind's role as 'vice-regent' and regards human beings as trustees for the rest of creation.[2] Freedom is a necessary aspect of the whole human being as God has created him or her.

Humankind's fall from grace, however, brings an end to this freedom. Servitude, oppression and exploitation are a necessary consequence of the Fall. Freedom is never regarded as absolute in the Scriptures; it is always subject to God and to his sovereign Law. Fallen human beings, however, put themselves in God's place and attempt to exercise sovereignty over their fellows. But their usurpation of power is characterized by a notable lack of integrity and justice—the very qualities which characterize divine sovereignty. The righteousness of God (*sedāqāh* in the Old Testament, *dikaiosunē* in the New Testament) affirms God's integrity, in the act of creation as well as his moral relation with humankind. This is in contrast to many pagan beliefs. God in the Bible is contrasted with the 'godlings' of the nations who have made humankind for sport and cannot be expected to be just in their dealings with human beings.

God is just in his dealings with humankind, but he also requires them to be just in their dealings with their fellow human beings. Both the Old and New Testament speak of God justifying the sinner on the basis of faith, but this justification, if it is not to become mere legal fiction, must restore just relations between human beings.[3] It is characteristic of the natural human being that such justice is not to be found in his relations with his fellow human beings. The absence of this justice is seen in interpersonal relationships where personal power may be expressed in oppressive and exploitative ways. Equally, injustice is found in the social structures which fallen humankind has created for itself. Tyrannies throughout the course of history bear witness to this extreme lack of justice. Structural and personal injustice often go hand in hand: oppressive power exercised by an individual is often supported by unjust socio-economic systems. In Asia, for example, personal dictatorships are nearly always maintained by feudal-military axes. The latter may in turn be strengthened by the relationship.

Social systems are not only oppressive when they support and are supported by a personal dictatorship. Their very structure may be oppressive in character and may reflect and perpetuate the division between the powerful and the powerless, the exploiters and the exploited. The caste system in India is an example of a social structure which has been developed to perpetuate the power-relations which exist between victor and vanquished. Military superiority has been transformed by this feat of social engineering into socio-economic hegemony.

Unequal power relations are expressed at the international as well as at the national level. The North-South divide places power and economic muscle with one group of nations at the expense of the other. The 'deification' of market forces is having disastrous consequences for the social fabric of Northern countries, but its effects on the emerging economies of Asia, Africa and Latin America are catastrophic. There is no intrinsic morality in the marketplace, and the weak are continually being made weaker. The North creates demand and then controls it. The power of large trans-national firms is such that they can virtually dictate the price of commodities produced by the South. The collapse of prices in the international markets of certain basic commodities produced by the South can ruin the economies of whole countries. A relationship of dependence has been created and is being sustained. Dependence is a complex phenomenon, but some of its other characteristic features are as follows: demand is artificially created and sustained by the North to find outlets for goods in the South; indebtedness is perpetuated by the soft loan system (usually and outrageously called aid!); industrialization is directed more toward Western needs than the needs of the nations of the South; prestigious development projects which are inappropriate to local needs are encouraged (this often provides an outlet for Western technology and manpower, but at an unacceptably high cost for the poorer countries); ruling elites are corrupted. The way in which local initiative towards appropriate development is stunted may be illustrated in Bangladesh, where the development of an appropriate pharmaceutical industry is continually being obstructed by trans-national interests.

The use of ideologies as a means of manipulating power requires further attention. An ideological state, whether fascist or socialist, has populist appeal. However, power tends to be vested in a ruling elite (an intellectual vanguard, political bureaucrats and the armed forces). The perpetuation of the ideology (on which it is alleged that the existence of the state depends) results in the perpetuation of the power of the party and of those who have power within the party. The ordinary citizen (on behalf of whom the ideology has been promoted) is more and more marginalized, and, if he seeks change, oppressed. Heterodoxy becomes the main evil in society and is to be rooted out at all costs. Real social evils such as corruption, abuse of power, or inefficiency in bureaucratized and centralized industry are ignored.

At present we are witnessing the emergence of ideological states based on religious fundamentalism. The *Wahhābī* revolution in *Saʿūdī ʿArabia* created an ideological state in the last century. This state was and is based on a rigorist interpretation of Islām as given in the two primary sources of that religion: the *Qurʾān* and the *Sunnah* (the practice of the Prophet of Islām). Now there are other Muslim fundamentalist states, although the basis of their fundamentalism is somewhat different. For example, importance may be given to authoritative figures—an 'apostolic succession'—as the primary sources of their religion. Alternatively, importance may be attributed to the cultural or geographical homogeneity of a people.[4]

Religious fundamentalism of all kinds exploits people's innate conservatism. Power is ultimately wielded by a religious establishment which claims to have a monopoly in the interpretation and application of the sacred tradition. Power is sometimes gained with the help of the masses, who see in religious fundamentalism a 'third way' between capitalism and socialism, but it is maintained by an alliance of the clergy, the armed forces and the bureaucracy. In global geo-political terms, such regimes are tolerated and even supported to maintain 'balances' of power. In the Western democracies too, religious fundamentalism can be a powerful political force, and because of its appeal to the masses, can influence state policy in important respects. In the U.S.A., we see the rise of the 'Moral Majority' which is attempting to achieve this goal: seeking to influence not only matters of moral concern, but also political decision-making on issues of interest to its members.

One important effect of the rise of fundamentalism as a state ideology is the suppression of religious minorities. Just as politically fundamentalist ideology forbids political dissent, so religiously fundamentalist ideology discourages religious dissent. Political fundamentalist ideology often discourages religious belief too, as it can be an alternative source for the ordering of life and so is regarded as a danger to the state ideology. On the other hand, religious fundamentalism frequently suppresses political dissent, as its custodians regard themselves as possessors of a divinely revealed ideology to which there can be no alternative. Recently there have been serious cases of the violation of the human rights of minority groups by fundamentalist regimes. The religious beliefs of such groups have been vilified, their places of worship seized or demolished and many have been driven out of their homes or put in prison. These are surely matters of concern to all who love justice and tolerance?

Another aspect of repression which must concern the Christian is the particular mentality it creates in those who are repressed. Systematic economic exploitation, for example, creates a mentality where mistrust and suspicion become the basis for social relationships. This ultimately results in social fragmentation and psychological alienation. Other symptoms of a repressed mentality can be outward sycophancy, accompanied by inner hostility. This adversely affects the integration of an individual's personality. It may also result in 'communal schizophrenia'.[5]

What does the Gospel's offer of wholeness mean in a context of repression? The invitation of the Gospel to repentance and new life has been presented by Christians and Churches with a great deal of power, influence and money. The repressed have, therefore, tended to see the Church as one more institution seeking to exploit them. In some areas, such as Latin America, the Church has wielded considerable political and financial influence and is seen as an oppressive institution even by its own theologians! In Asia, the situation is somewhat different. Here a generally poor Church regards its leaders with mistrust as they are suspected (sometimes justifiably) of exploiting the poverty of their constituency for their own enrichment. The struggle to achieve and to maintain power in the Church is one of the greatest stumbling blocks to an effective proclamation of the Gospel to the poor.[6]

The vital link between God's justice and the justification of the sinner must again be emphasized. This must not be seen simply as a royal pardon—as a return to some kind of *tabula rasa*—but rather as the gradual creation of righteousness in the justified sinner. The justification of the sinner, his being accounted righteous, must result in his being made just: this in turn should result in an effort to establish justice in the Christian's social, political and economic environment.[7]

Gospel principles need to be kept in mind in the Christian's witness for justice and against injustice. First, a Christian is forbidden to employ violent means to safeguard his or her own rights.[8] Second, he or she is to obey secular authority only 'insofar as the Law of Christ allows'. In other words, where secular authority attempts to usurp God's place or to violate his law, obedience is not mandatory. The refusal of the early Christians to ascribe divine titles to Caesar or to sacrifice to the gods are an example of this kind of Godly disobedience. The Christian (or a group of Christians) cannot, therefore, struggle for their own rights, but they may rightly struggle for the rights of other (Christian and non-Christian) oppressed groups. The Christian, in keeping with the whole of prophetic and dominical tradition, may witness for justice in a situation where there is oppression and exploitation.[9] Identification and an expression of solidarity with the oppressed is an area of Christian concern which has attracted considerable attention in recent years.

The most effective commendation of the Gospel, in many contexts, comes from those who are powerless in worldly terms but have found new life in Jesus Christ to be a profound source of power for living and loving. The Base Ecclesial Communities in many parts of the world, ministries of identification with and care for the poor, the emergence of theologies which take the question of justice seriously, are all signs that such a commendation of the Gospel is taking place in some contexts. There are numerous Christian communities throughout the Third World whose main aim is to live with the poor, experience their suffering and offer the Gospel to them in word and deed. Such communities are transforming the Church's understanding of her own mission and also compelling a cynical world to take the Church more seriously. The Christian doctrine of the Incarnation provides a theological basis for the Church's involvement with the poor in this way.[10]

Christians should affirm and stand with all those who seek justice and truth. They should acknowledge as effective 'signs of the Kingdom' all efforts to establish justice and to do away with exploitation and greed. They should endeavour to work with all people of good will, whatever their belief or lack of belief, who seek to promote a more just and humane world.[11]

The Gospel's offer of wholeness to humanity involves more than social action; it includes a further dimension of spiritual healing. Such healing is concerned with all aspects of life. It should bring integration of personality, mental stability and experience of salvation along with physical healing. An area that is much emphasized today is the healing of relationships. Christians as a community should show marks of restoration and wholeness in their communal life. This is a powerful witness to the world.

One of the most exciting developments in theology in recent years has been the recovery of the biblical teaching that God suffers with and for us. He is compassionate in the strict sense. God's suffering is not simply compassionate, however, it is also redemptive. Divine involvement with human suffering has a purpose—the elimination of suffering. God comes to us in our situation to save us from our predicament.[12] The Church, in continuing its mission, is also called to suffering. Certainly such suffering refines Christian character, but it should also be a means for the redemption of the world.[13] Identification with the oppressed is not enough—there must be a proclamation of the Kingdom and its values, such a humble service and such a commitment to Gospel truth that the poor are saved in every sense of the word; saved not only from outside oppression and exploitation but saved from their own ignorance and brokenness. In other words saved from their own sin.

NOTES TO CHAPTERS

INTRODUCTION

1 I owe the term to Prof. L. Sanneh, Associate Professor at the Centre for the Study of World Religions at Harvard.
2 See further the present writer's, *Islām: A Christian Perspective,* Paternoster (UK), Westminster (USA), p. 153f.
3 See further J. Sobrino, *Christology at the Crossroads,* Orbis 1978; also R. Padilla, 'Christology and Mission in the Two Thirds World', in *Sharing Jesus in the Two Thirds World* (eds. V. Samuel and C. Sugden), Bangalore, 1983.
4 *Towards a New Relationship,* Epworth Press, 1986, p. 29.
5 For a history of the Oriental Orthodox, see A. Atiya, *Eastern Christianity,* London, 1949.
6 See further D. Lacey O'Leary, *How Greek Science Passed to the Arabs,* London, 1949.
7 The title of a recent consultation organized by the Christian Conference of Asia.

PART 1: Chapter 1

1 See further the present writer's, *Islām: A Christian Perspective;* De Lacey O'Leary, *How Greek Science Passed to the Arabs;* and R. Walzer, *Greek into Arabic,* Oxford, 1962.
2 Bell, R., *The Origin of Islām in its Christian Environment,* London, 1926, p. 53f.
3 *M. J. Nazir-Ali,* op. cit., pp. 26–27.
4 *Maulānā Abū Aʿlā Maudūdī, Towards Understanding Islām,* Lahore, 1978, p. 97.
5 Ibid., p. 94; Bowker. J., *The Problem of Suffering in the Religions of the World,* CUP, 1970, p. 127.
6 *Nazir-Ali,* 'A Christian Approach to Islām', in *Jesus Christ the Only Way* (ed. P. Sookhdeo), Paternoster, 1978, p. 78f.

7 See further Sahas, D. J., *John of Damascus on Islām*, Leiden, 1972.
8 Cf. Chapter 2, 'Christology in an Islāmic Context.'
9 See Kraemer, H., *Religion and the Christian Faith*, London, 1956.
10 See for example, Rudvin, A., 'The Gospel and Islām: What Sort of Dialogue is Possible?', *Al-Mushir*, Rawalpindi, Autumn 1979, pp. 94–95.
11 Ibid., pp. 114–115.
12 Ibid., p. 115.
13 'Islāmic Theology: Limits and Bridges' in *The Gospel and Islām* (ed. D. M. McCurry), Monrovia, 1979, p. 198.
14 See Paul Avis, 'Luther's Theology of the Church', in *The Churchman*, 1983, No. 2, p. 104f.
15 Rudvin's point about the inscrutability of God in Islām is well taken: op. cit., p. 113.
16 'Islām and Incarnation' in J. Hick (ed.), *Truth and Dialogue*, London, 1974, p. 126f.
17. See Chapter 2, 'Christology in an Islāmic Context'.
18 2 Peter 1:4 and Athanasius, *De Incarnatione*.
19 *Iqbāl's* particular merit is that he recognizes the dependence of this fatalism on a particular doctrine of God: *The Reconstruction of Religious Thought in Islām'*, Oxford 1934, Lahore 1971, p. 110f.
20 In this connection see Margaret Smith's splendid and seminal work, *Studies in Early Mysticism in the Near and Middle East*, London, 1931; also, *M. Iqbāl, The Development of Metaphysics in Persia*, Lahore, 1964; p. 76f.
21 See further Zwemer, S., *The Moslem Christ*, London, 1912.
22 *M. Iqbāl*, 'Metaphysics . . .', p. 87f.; *Jalāluddīn Rūmī, Diwān-i-Shams-i-Tabrīz* (ed. R. A. Nicholson), Cambridge, 1898.
23 *Nazir-Ali, Islām: A Christian Perspective*, op. cit, p. 66f.
24 *Payām-i-Mashriq*, Lahore, 1923, p. 30.
25 In this connection see Chapter 4, 'The Place of Holy Scripture in Muslim-Christian Dialogue.'

PART I: Chapter 2

1 For an example see *Mahmoud M. Ayoub*, 'Towards an Islāmic Christology: An image of Jesus in early Shī-ʿī Muslim Literature', *Muslim World*, July, 1976.
2 *M. Iqbāl, The Reconstruction of Religious Thought in Islām*, p. 62f.
3 A. Rudvin, 'The Gospel and Islām: What Sort of Dialogue is Possible?', p. 101.
4 *Rūmī, Fīhi mā Fīhi*, Teheran, 1959, p. 148f.
5 R. C. Zaehner, *At Sundry Times*, London, Faber and Faber, 1958.
6 *Epistle to the Ephesians* 1:1, 18:2, Smyrn. 6:1, cf. Acts 20:28.
7 e.g. J. Moltmann, *The Crucified God*, London, SCM, 1974.
8 *Jāvīd-Nāma*, Lahore, 1974, p. 38.
9 Rudvin, op. cit., p. 98.
10 Op. cit., 7:2.

11 Magn. 7:2, 8:2.
12 For a Christian interpretation of *Qur'ānic* Christology see G. Bassetti-Sani's highly controversial book, *The Koran in the Light of Christ*, Chicago, Franciscan Herald, 1977.
13 K. Cragg, 'Islām and Incarnation' in *Truth and Dialogue* (ed. J. Hick), p. 126f; cf. Chapter 1, pp. 19–20.
14 *Disputation against the Saracens*, Migne's ed., cf. Patriarch Timothy's dialogue with the *Caliph Al-Mahdi* in W. G. Young, *Patriarch, Shah and Caliph*, Rawalpindi, Christian Study Centre, 126B, Murree Road, 1974, Appendix D, p. 198ff.
15 H. Wehr, *A Dictionary of Modern Written Arabic*, London, Allen and Unwin, 1971, p. 838.
16 Q. 3:59.
17 *A. Yusuf 'Ali, Text, Translation and Commentary on the Holy Qur'ān*, Leicester, Islāmic Book Depot, 1975.
18 R. C. Zaehner, *At Sundry Times*, London, Faber and Faber, 1958, and G. Parrinder, *Jesus in the Qur'ān*, London, Faber and Faber, 1965.
19 Parrinder, op. cit., p. 105.
20 Q. 3:55, 4:157.
21 For a summing up see my *Islām: A Christian Perspective*, p. 17f.
22 T. Andrae, *Moḥammed: The Man and his Faith*, London, Allen and Unwin, 1936, p. 191.

PART 1: Chapter 3

1 Q. 17:85 cf. *M. Iqbāl, The Reconstruction of Religious Thought in Islām*, Lahore, 1971, p. 103.
2 See further C. K. Barrett, *The Gospel according to St. John*, London, 1967, p. 127f.
3 Cf. C. F. D. Moule, *The Origins of Christology*, CUP 1977: Moule stresses the point that the definite article is often used in the expression 'The Son of Man' in the New Testament, and that this implies that a special being is being referred to here. Without the article, that phrase might have meant 'a human being'; but with it, it definitely refers to the divine man of Jewish apocalyptic.
4 Ignatius, *Epistle to the Ephesians* 7:2.
5 A phrase much used in modern Latin American theology, see for example J. Sobrino, *Christology at the Cross Roads*, Orbis, 1878; R. Padilla, 'Christology and Mission in the Two Thirds World', in *Sharing Jesus in the Two Thirds World* (eds. V. Samuel and C. Sugden), p. 17f.
6 G. S. Hendry, 'Christology' in *A Dictionary of Christian Theology* (ed. A. Richardson), SCM, 1969, p. 57f.
7 See H. Chadwick, *The Early Church*, London, 1967, p. 202f.
8 Paulos Gregorios, W. H. Lazareth and N. A. Nissiotis (eds.), *Does Chalcedon Divide or Unite?*, Geneva, 1981.
9 Ibid., 128f.
10 Ibid., p. 43.

11 Chadwick, *The Early Church*, p. 197.
12 *Does Chalcedon Divide or Unite?*, p. 62; cf. 1 Cor. 2:8 and Acts 3:15.
13 W. G. Young, *Patriarch, Shah and Caliph*, pp. 197, 200, 205, Rawalpindi 1974.
14 Chadwick, p. 192.
15 See, for example, the Hymns and Homilies of Ephraim Syrus (*Library of Nicene and Post-Nicene Fathers*, Vol. XIII, p. 115f) and the writings of the Egyptian Desert Fathers such as St. Anthony (see Migne XL 961f.), and the life of Abba Pishoi (Eng. Tr., Chicago, ND).
16 Ignatius, *Epistle to the Ephesians* 20:2; Chadwick, p. 198.
17 See *Tahāfut Al-Falāsifa*, Beirut, 1927.
18 M. S. Seale, *Muslim Theology*, London, 1964.
19 *Nazir-Ali, Islām: A Christian Perspective*, 1983, for a detailed discussion of John's relation to Islām. See D. J. Sahas, *John of Damascus on Islām*.
20 W. G. Young, op. cit., p. 198f.
21 De Lacey O'Leary, *How Greek Science passed to the Arabs*.
22 K. Kitamori, *Theology of the Pain of God*, Richmond, Virginia, USA, 1965; cf. J. Moltmann, *The Crucified God*, London, 1974.
23 For example, Minjung theology; cf. the collection *Minjung Theology* (ed. K. Y. Bock), Singapore, 1981.
24 Especially, of course, the Psalms in *Punjābi*.
25 I have in mind, in our own context, the work of such poets as *Ẓiā*, *Ṣarf Clarkābādī, A. R. Nāẓim, Mushtāq Inʿāmī* and others. Bishop Lesslie Newbigin's remark regarding Tamil devotional literature is relevant here too, 'Anyone who has lived within the Tamil Churches knows that there are rich resources of living Christian faith and experience embodied in the continuing stream of Tamil Christian lyrical poetry, a stream which has flowed for a century and a half and is still flowing, strongly. The people who write, read and sing these lyrics do not take any part in the ecumenical movement. Their lyrics cannot be translated into a European language without losing their power and beauty. The world of thought, the concepts through which they capture and express the deepest Christian experiences are not those which appear in the documents of ecumenical meetings.' See also Newbigin's criticism that most Third-World theologies are reflections of Western concerns, *The Open Secret*, London, 1978, p. 170f.

PART I: Chapter 4

1 See further the present writer's, 'A Christian approach to Islām' in P. Sookhdeo (ed.), *Jesus Christ: The Only Way*, p. 79f., cf. Chapter 1, p. 17.
2 *Maulana A. Yusufʿ Alī, The Holy Qur'ān*: Text, Trans. and Commentary, Leicester, 1975, p. 46f., n. 107.
3 See further the present writer's *Islām: A Christian Perspective*, p. 22; J. De Hart, *Taḥrīf in Early Islām*, Communicators' Fellowship, 1982, unpublished.

4 There is, of course, a tradition within Islām which has regarded the *Qur'ān* as culture-specific. The so-called Islāmic philosophers *Ibn Rushd* (Averroes) and *Ibn Sīnā* (Avicenna) would fall into this category. In more modern times, the eighteenth century theologian *Shāh Walīullah* of Delhi and *'Allāma Iqbāl* (d. 1938) both regarded the penal law of the *Qur'ān* as culture-specific and not necessarily binding on all cultures at all times. See further *M. J. Nazir-Ali,* op. cit., p. 70f., 82; *Shāh Walīullah, Ḥujjatullāh Al Bāligha,* Vol. 1, Lahore, 1979, p. 220f.; cf. *G. N. Jalbani, The Teachings of Shāh Walīullah,* Lahore, 1967, p. 92f.; *'Allāma Iqbāl, The Reconstruction of Religious Thought in Islām,* p. 171f.

5 See, for example, Timothy of Baghdād's use of this argument to counter the charge of altering the Scriptures made by the *Caliph Mahdī,* W. G. Young, *Patriarch Shah and Caliph,* p. 202.

6 There is, however, some evidence that the recension of *Ibn Mas'ūd* survived for a good many years after the promulgation of the *'Uthmānic* recension. Some *Shī-'a* also claim *taḥrīf* of the *Qur'ān* in the *'Uthmānic* version. Their charge is that sections to do with the Imamate of *'Alī* have been omitted. See further *Nazir-Ali,* op. cit., p. 42f.; *Iqbāl, The Reconstruction,* p. 175.

7 We are fortunate to have a masterly contribution in *Urdū* on this issue in Archdeacon *Barkat Ullah's 'Ṣaḥat-e-Kutb-e-Muqdassa,* Lahore, 1968.

8 *Tafhīm Al-Qur'ān,* Vol. 1, Lahore, 1973, pp. 231–232.

9 *Nazir-Ali,* op. cit. p. 13f.; J. Slomp, *Pseudo-Barnabas in the Context of Muslim-Christian Apologetic,* Rawalpindi, 1974.

10 R. Bell, *The Origin of Islām in its Christian Environment,* London, 1968; J. De Hart, op. cit.

11 It is interesting to see that Timothy and his interlocutor refer to the four canonical Gospels and that Timothy defends the integrity of these Gospels. The Church has never tried to replace these with a 'Gospel harmony', even though manuscripts of an Arabic version of the *Diatessaron* exist. See Young, op. cit., p. 201. Sometimes, however, Gospel harmonies are produced for catechetical purposes. The latest of these is a fine version produced in Persian called *'Injīl-i-Masīḥ'.* Another in Arabic, called *'Sīral-Al-Masīh'* has just been published.

12 M. S. Seale, *Muslim Theology,* p. 69; R. Bell, op. cit., p. 209f.

13 *Nazir-Ali,* op. cit., p. 15f.

14 D. J. Sahas, *John of Damascus on Islām,* p. 152; Seale, op. cit., *passim;* R. Bell, op. cit., p. 209f.

15 See further Seale, op. cit., p. 74f.; *Iqbāl, The Development of Metaphysics in Persia,* Lahore, 1954.

16 *Professor Faẓl ur Raḥmān* is a name that comes readily to mind.

17 J. De Hart, op. cit.

18 *Barkat Ullah* makes this point repeatedly, op. cit., p. 70 and *passim.*

19 See further K. A. Kitchen, *Ancient Orient and Old Testament,* Illinois, 1966; E. Yamauchi, *The Stones and the Scriptures,* London, 1972; *Barkat Ullah,* op. cit., p. 75f.

20 In this connection see Professor James Dunn's seminal article 'The Authority of Scripture, According to Scripture', in *The Churchman,* London, 1982, vols. II and III.

21 Madras, 1898.
22 This paper was written for a Bible Society Consultation on Ministry in West Asia, South Asia and Indonesia in 1983.

PART I: Chapter 5

1 *Zabūr-i-ʿAjam,* Lahore, 1927 (reprinted 1970), p. 160; *Bāl-i-Jibra'il,* p. 54; and *Rumi's Dīwān* (ed. R. A. Nicholson), CUP, 1898, Lahore, 1936, Tabrīz ed, 1280 A.H.
2 *Reconstruction of Religious Thought in Islām,* p. 124f.
3 *Payām-i-Mashriq,* p. 207.
4 Ibid., p. 197 cf. *Gulshan-i-Rāz-i-Jadīd,* (*Zabūr-i-ʿAjam,* p. 221).
5 *Ḥakīm Sanā'Ī, Ḥadīqat al-Ḥaqīqat* (ed. J. Stephenson), Wellingborough, 1968, p. 1, line 12, Lahore, 1932, reprint 1974; *Jalāluddīn Rūmī, Fīhi mā Fīhi,* Teheran, 1959, p. 240f.
6 op. cit., p. 46f.
7 *Ideals and Realities of Islām,* London, 1966, p. 27.
8 *Jāvīd-Nāma,* Lahore, 1932, p. 39.
9 For a detailed discussion of Christian terminology in *Iqbāl,* see *Nazīr Yusuf, Iqbāl Aur Masīḥī Iṣṭilāḥāt,* Lahore, 1978.
10 *Bāng-i-Darā,* Lahore, 1924, p. 264.
11 *Zabūr-i-ʿAjam,* p. 136.
12 *Bāng-i-Darā,* p. 280; cf. *Yusuf* op. cit., p. 75f.
13 *Payām,* p. 30; cf. Chapter 1, pp. 20–2.
14 *Qur'ān* 7:143, 20:10f; cf. Ex. 3:1–6, 19:16f; 33:18f.
15 *Jāvīd-Nāma* p. 52. A lamp is often used as a symbol for incarnation in Islām (see for example, *Ṣūfī* interpretations of the light verse in the *Qur'ān* 24:35). The title 'Son of Mary' in Islām points to the virgin birth and Jesus' uniqueness in this respect. See further G. Parrinder, *Jesus in the Qur'ān*, London, 1965, ch. 3.
16 See, nevertheless, the reductionist note of the editors. *Jāvīd-Nāma,* p. 53.
17 *Zabūr-i-ʿAjam,* p. 72.
18 See further the present writer's *Islām: A Christian Perspective,* p. 66f. Also, S. Zwemer, *The Moslem Christ,* London, 1912, and A. Rudvin, 'A Supplementary note to a List of the Appellations of the Prophet *Muḥammad*', *Muslim World,* LXVIII, No. 1, 1978, p. 57f.
19 *Rumūz-i-Bēkhūdī,* Lahore, 1918, p. 130. *Iqbāl* is paraphrasing here a tradition about the Prophet which is: 'I was a Prophet while Adam was between water and clay'.
20 *Jāvīd-Nāma,* p. 128–129. 'Except God' is an allusion to a part of the *Kalima,* the Muslim profession of faith, 'There is no God except God'.
21 Ibid., p. 52.
22 Ibid., p. 49. *Ahriman* is the principle of evil in the Zoroastrian system, here equated with the devil. 'The saw' refers to the sawing apart of Zechariah, 'the worm' to Job and the cross to Jesus.
23 *Qur'ān* 2:61, 91.
24 Quoted in *Jāvīd-Nāma,* p. 117.

25 See further the present writer's *Christology in an Islāmic Context*, p. 34–5; K. Cragg, *Jesus and the Muslim*, London, 1985, p. 63.
26 *Reconstruction*. 116.
27 *Qur'ān* 22:5, 86:8–12.
28 *Reconstruction*, p. 116.
29 e.g. *Sūrah* 112. *Reconstruction*, p. 62f.
30 Ibid., p. 71f.
31 See, for example, *Patriarch, Shah and Caliph*, Appendix D, p. 198f.
32 R. Bell, *The Origin of Islām in its Christian Environment;* A. Geiger, *Judaism and Islām;* M. S. Seale, *Muslim Theology.*
33 Seale, op. cit., p. 30f.
34 *The Development of Metaphysics in Persia*, p. 41f., 52f.; *Nazir-Ali, Islām: A Christian Perspective*, op. cit., p. 73f.
35 See also the present writer's *Islām: A Christian Perspective*, p. 73f.

[The joint edition of *Bāng-i-Darā*, *Ḍarb-i-Kalīm* and *Bāl-i-Jibra'il* is used in quotations. Also, quotations from the *Asrār* and *Rumūz* are from the joint edition (last reprint 1969).]

PART II: **Introduction**

1 *For the Sake of the Kingdom: God's Church and the New Creation*, Inter-Anglican Theological and Doctrinal Commission, ACC, London, 1986, p. 35.
2 See further K. Cracknell, *Towards a New Relationship: Christians and People of Other Faiths*, p. 101f.
3 Sir Norman Anderson, *God's Law and Love*, Collins, 1980, pp. 32–3, 128.

PART II: Chapter 6

1 J. H. Newman, *Apologia pro Vita Sua*, London, 1959, p. 178, cf. Eph. 2:12.
2 See for example J. W. Sweetman, *Islām and Christian Theology*, Vol. 1, London, 1945, p. 62 and *passim*. There are exceptions to this however; some Muslim theologians have held to a doctrine of Hereditary Sin (see A. J. Wensinck, *The Muslim Creed*, London, 1965, p. 137). Also, there is a famous tradition that the Prophet of Islām said, 'No child is born but the devil hath touched it, except Mary and her son Jesus.'
3 London, 1968, p. 124.
4 See for example, Romans Ch. 1–3; cf. Ps. 14:1–3, 51:5, 53:1–3.
5 The classic work on the biblical view of the human will is of course Luther's *The Bondage of the Will*, London, 1957. One need not go all the way with Luther to realize the fact of the slavery of Man's will, potentially free, to sin. One highly original way of conflating the 'physico-chemical' and the 'volitional' view of the origin of moral evil is

to hold that original sin is Man's inherited animal nature which continually strives to achieve mastery over his ethical and religious consciousness. Animal nature is not in itself sinful, but where it is allowed free expression over and above the demands of conscience, it is then recognized as sinful. Such a view is increasingly popular among scientists who are Christians. See R. Stannard, *Science and the Renewal of Belief*, SCM, 1982.

6 See Kant, *Religion Within the Limits of Reason Alone*, New York, 1960.
7 Gen. 3:17–19; Rom. 8:19–22.
8 See further F. W. Dillistone, *The Christian Understanding of Atonement*, Nisbet, 1968.
9 *Rūmī, Fīhi mā Fīhi*, p. 96; Q 7:172, 2:156.
10 J. Moltmann, *Man*, SPCK, London, 1974, p. 46f.; J. Bowker, *Problems of Suffering in the Religions of the World*, CUP, 1970, p. 137f.
11 Moltmann, op. cit., p. 52.
12 Indeed, Prof. H. D. Lewis, in a lecture at Lahore Cathedral entitled 'Solitude in Modern Literature' has shown that loneliness is a dominant concern in much modern English literature.
13 S. Zwemer, *The Moslem Christ*, London, 1912, p. 155f.
14 Ps. 51:16, 17; Amos 5:21–24; Joel 2:13.
15 Phil. 2:5–11; 2 Cor. 5:18; Heb. 1:1–4.
16 Heb. 2:10; 12:2.
17 Rom. 5:15–21.
18 Mt. 24:14; Jn. 3:16; Rom. 10:18; 11:32; Col. 1:20; 1 Tim. 4:10.
19 See further J. A. T. Robinson, *Wrestling with Romans*, SCM, 1979.
20 C. S. Lewis, *The Great Divorce*, Glasgow, 1972. In this connection it may be worth pointing out that certain strands in the Indian Mystical tradition emphasize the increasing isolation of the liberated soul and give positive value to it. Cf. C. R. C. Zachner, *Mysticism: Sacred and Profane*, OUP, 1961, p. 98f.
21 Such Universalism is present even in the Old Testament, e.g. in Deutero-Isaiah, Jonah, Micah, and some of the Psalms.
22 *Church Dogmatics II, The Doctrine of God*, 2, ET, Edinburgh, 1959; cf. Eph. 1:4.
23 Genesis 14:18–20; Ps. 67; Is. 45; Acts 14:16, 17; 17:22–31.
24 Mt. 5:17f.; 22:41–46.
25 John 4:42.
26 C. K. Barrett, *The Gospel according to St. John*, London, 1967, p. 204.
27 Romans 13:1–7; 1 Peter 2:13–17.

PART II : Chapter 7

1 I. H. Marshall, *The Gospel of Luke*, Exeter, 1978, p. 813.
2 For example, N. Saracco, 'The Liberating Options of Jesus' in *Sharing Jesus in the Two Thirds World*, (eds. V. Samuel and C. Sugden), p. 57f.
3 See J. D. Yoder, *The Politics of Jesus*, Grand Rapids, 1972.

4 For the work of a deacon in relieving need, see H. Chadwick, *The Early Church*, p. 46f.
5 C. K. Barrett, *The Gospel according to St. John*, p. 366.
6 Archbishop Henry D'Souza of India. Quoted in 'Focus' (a journal of pastoral theology), B. Mendes, *The Asian Church*, Jan. 1984, p. 15.
7 J. Bowker, *The Problem of Suffering in the Religions of the World*, CUP, 1970, p. 143f.
8 Chadwick, op. cit., p. 47f.
9 An excellent book produced by the Diocese of Lahore, *Serving Community*, usefully summarizes this role of the Church (Lahore, 1983).
10 See further, K. Y. Bock (ed.), *Minjung Theology*, Singapore, 1981, p. 21f.
11 'The Exhortations' before Holy Communion, *The Book of Common Prayer*, Church of India, Pākistān, Burma and Ceylon, p. 342.
12 See further R. J. Foster, *Celebration of Discipline*, London, 1981.
13 From a Persian *ghazal* by the present writer. There is a play on words here: *Nazir* means warner, whereas *Bashir* means a bearer of good news.

PART II: Chapter 8

1 In this connection, see a fascinating book by Seppo Syrjanen, *In Search of Meaning and Identity*, Helsinki, 1984.
2 A. Thiselton, *The Two Horizons*, Paternoster, 1980, N. D. Osborn, *Principles of Dynamic Equivalence*, place and date of publication unknown.
3 See the present writer's *Islām: A Christian Perspective;* Margaret Smith, *Studies in Early Mysticism in the Near and Middle East;* M. S. Seale, *Muslim Theology;* D. J. Sahas, *John of Damascus on Islām*.
4 In Pākistān, the most well-known instānce of this is All Saint's Church, Peshawar.
5 The Urdū Bible uses the word *Allāh* in 1 Chr. 6:48. The ordinary word for God is, however, the Persian *Khudā* or the Arabic *Ilah*.
6 See for example, R. D. Winter, 'The Highest Priority: Cross-Cultural Evangelism', in *The Church in New Frontiers for Missions*, D. A. Fraser (ed.), Monrovia, 1983, p. 94.
7 *Nazir-Ali*, op. cit., p. 13f.; Bell, op. cit., p. 90f.
8 For the debate on contextualization, see further Bruce J. Nicholls, *Contextualization: A Theology of Gospel and Culture*, Paternoster, 1979; *The Willow Bank Report: Gospel and Culture*, Singapore, 1978.

PART II: Chapter 9

1 In this chapter, examples are drawn from the experiences of those at the Cathedral Church of the Resurrection in Lahore.
2 WCC Muslim-Christian meeting, Chambésy, 1979, p. 1.

3 This is what the Lausanne Covenant means by dialogue. See further John R. W. Stott's *The Lausanne Covenant—an Exposition and Commentary*, Wheaton, 1975, p. 12.
4 See, for example, Chapter 2, 'Christology in an Islāmic Context'; D. Brown, 'The Divine Trinity' in *Christianity and Islām 4*, SPCK, London, 1969; and Archdeacon *Barkat Ullah's, Ṣaḥat-e-Kutb-e-Muqadassa*, Lahore, 1968.
5 op. cit., p. 1, No. 7.
6 L. A. Yuzon, 'Communicating the Christian Message', CCA, preparatory paper, N.D., p. 55f.
7 *Christian Witness to Muslims*, LCWE, Wheaton, 1980, p. 21f.; see further the present writer's *Islām: A Christian Perspective*, p. 145f.
8 H. Chadwick, *The Early Church*, p. 47f. For an instance of the early Church's attitude to the poor, see D. F. Winslow, 'Gregory of Nazianzus and Love for the Poor', *Anglican Theological Review*, Oct. 1965, p. 348f.
9 Since this was written, an independent organization called Christian Development Foundation has been established which is seeking to bring about a change in the lives of the brick-kiln workers.
10 *Report on the Consultation on the Relationship between Evangelism and Social Responsibility*, Paternoster, 1982, p. 21f.
11 Quoted in the Centennial Souvenir of the Salvation Army in Pākistān, Lahore, 1983, p. 3.
12 op. cit., p. 22.
13 1 Cor. 12:27f., Rom. 12:4.

PART II: Chapter 10

1 Some of them are set out in Colin Buchanan and others, *Growing into Union*, London, 1970.
2 As a parallel, the revival of this form of Church Government in the Roman Catholic Church is worthy of note. See Hans Kung, *The Changing Church*, London, 1965, p. 20f.
3 Executive Committee Minute Ex-C-37-83, Ex-C-43-83. See also Appendix A of the minutes.
4 *Plan of Union* (4th edn.), 1965.
5 In this connection, see Chapters 2 & 3.
6 Constitution of the Church of Pākistān, XA p. 20, Lahore, 1973.
7 See especially the materials produced for the CWME Conference 'Your Kingdom Come', particularly Bulletin No. 12, March 1980. Also the official publication *Your Kingdom Come: Mission Perspectives*, Geneva, 1980.
8 *Traditional Christology in an Asian Context*, Ch. 3, see p. 42. L. Newbigin, *The Open Secret*, London, 1978, p. 170f.
9 See further the present writer's, *Islām: A Christian Perspective*, p. 142f.
10 Ibid., p. 156f.
11 *Nazir-Ali, Islām: A Christian Perspective*, p. 126f.; *Abu Aʿlā Maudūdī, Rights of Non Muslims in an Islāmic State*, Lahore, 1961.

PART III: **Introduction**

1 See the present writer's *Islām: A Christian Perspective*, p. 145–150; also Kenneth Cracknell, *Towards a New Relationship: Christians and People of other Faiths*, Epworth, 1986, Ch. 2.
2 British Council of Churches, *Relations with People of Other Faiths: Guidelines on Dialogue in Britain*, 1981.

PART III: Chapter 11

1 H. Kraemer, *Religion and the Christian Faith*, London, 1956.
2 J. Hick, *God and the Universe of Faiths*, Macmillan, 1973.
3 W. Freytag, *The Gospel and the Religions*, SCM, 1957.
4 F. W. Dillistone, *The Christian Understanding of Atonement*.
5 L. S. Thornton, *Revelation and the Modern World*, London, 1950.
6 *The Ruling Class*, Act 1, scene 4, London, 1969.
7 Prayer in the name of Jesus and to Jesus are early aspects of Christian worship. See further, O. Cullmann, *Early Christian Worship*, London, 1953 and *Christology of the New Testament*, London, 1959, p. 214f.

PART III: Chapter 12

1 S. J. Samartha, *The Hindū Response to the Unbound Christ*, Madras, 1974. See also M. M. Thomas, *The Acknowledged Christ of the Indian Renaissance*, London, 1969.
2 V. Samuel and C. Sugden (eds.), *The Gospel Among our Hindū Neighbours*, Bangalore, 1983, p. 201f.
3 *Nazir-Ali, Islām: A Christian Perspective*, p. 145f.
4 George Bebawi, 'The Future of Christianity in the Middle East', CMS inter-change partner, unpublished paper, 1985.
5 The latest example of this, of course, is the BMU's excellent report, *Towards a Theology for Inter-faith Dialogue*, London, 1984.
6 See further G. Parrinder, *Jesus in the Qur'ān*, London, 1965.
7 In different ways, the following two books illustrate this point: Bede Griffiths, *The Marriage of East and West*, London, 1983; and V. Samuel and C. Sugden (eds.), op. cit.
8 D. Kwang-Sun Suh, 'Minjung and Theology in Korea', in *Minjung Theology*, ed. K. Y. Bock, Singapore, 1981, p. 17f.
9 See, for example, A. Rudvin, 'The Gospel and Islām; What Sort of Dialogue is Possible?', *Al-Mushir*, Autumn 1979, Rawalpindi, p. 94f.
10 Ninian Smart uses the term 'conceptual fideism' to indicate a position which holds that to understand a faith properly one must belong to it, in J. Hick (ed.), *Truth and Dialogue*, London, 1974, p. 52f.
11 K. Cragg, *Muḥammad and the Christian: A Question of Response*, New York and London, 1984, p. 12f.

12 Rudvin, op. cit., p. 111f.; but see the treatment given to this doctrine by Kenneth Cracknell in *Towards A New Relationship: Christians and People of Other Faith*, p. 100f. It seems clear, however, that Cracknell has not been able to establish that the Fathers teach the presence of the seminal word in other *religions*.
13 BMU report, op. cit., pp. 24–26.
14 op. cit., p. 112.
15 op. cit., pp. 16–17.
16 op. cit., pp. 25–26. Any notion of earning salvation, particularly through religious practices, must be carefully excluded. See further C. Sugden, *Christ's Exclusive Claims and Inter-faith Dialogue*, Nottingham, 1985, pp. 13–14 (quoting Sir Norman Anderson).
17 K. Barth, *Church Dogmatics II, The Doctrine of God*, ET, Edinburgh, 1959; cf. Eph. 1:4.
18 *Epistle to the Ephesians*, 7: 2, London, 1954.
19 Rudvin, op. cit., p. 116f.
20 op. cit., p. 20.

PART III : Chapter 13

1 R. Bell, *The Origin of Islām in its Christian Environment*, p. 907.
2 *A. Yusuf ʿAli, The Holy Qur'ān*. Text, trans., comm., p. 1306. See also p. 314.
3 A. Geiger, *Judaism and Islām*, p. 301.
4 Bell, op. cit., p. 17.
5 M. M. Pickthall, *The Meaning of the Glorious Qur'ān*, New York, N.D., p. 133.
6 *Ẓafarullah Khan, The Qur'ān*, Text and trans., London, 1975, p. 158.
7 See Chapter 4, 'The Place of Holy Scripture in Muslim-Christian Encounter'; and the present author's *Islām: A Christian Perspective*, p. 13f.
8 Bell, op. cit., p. 138.
9 'Islām and Incarnation' in *Truth and Dialogue*, ed. John Hick.
10 Geiger, op. cit., p. 39.
11 G. Basetti-Sani, *The Koran in the Light of Christ*.
12 *Fīhi mā Fīhi Maulānā Jalāluddīn Rūmī*, p. 148f.
13 Iqbāl, Zabūr-i-ʿ*Ajam*, Lahore 1927 (reprint 1970). p. 72.

PART IV: Chapter 14

1 'Islām as a Moral and Political Ideal', reprinted in *Thought and Reflections of Iqbāl*, Lahore, 1964, p. 52f. Muslims sometimes refer to their religion as *Dīn-i-Muḥamadiyya* (or religion of *Muḥammad*).
2 *Rumūz-i-Bēkhudī*, Lahore, 1969, p. 130.
3 *Jāvīd-Nāma*, p. 129 (but see whole context).

4 See 33:46 where *Muḥammad* is described as a bright lamp.
5 *Shahrastani*, edited by Cureton, London, 1846, p. 42.
6 Bishop A. Rudvin, basing himself on T. Andrae, reckons it is the most popular book after the *Qur'ān* in Muslim devotion. A supplementary note to 'A list of the Appellations of the Prophet *Muḥammad*,' *Muslim World*, LXVIII, No. 1, 1978, p. 57f.
7 *Muslim World*, LXVI, 1976, p. 259f.
8 S. P. Amin, the *Daily Sun*, March 23rd, 1979.
9 *Dalā'il Al-Khairāt*, Taj Company, Karachi, N.D., p. 83. I am greatly indebted to Bishop Rudvin for calling my attention to *Dalā'il Al-Khairāt*.
10 J. Wensinck, *The Muslim Creed*, 1932, p. 180. Also *A Dictionary of Comparative Religion*, ed. S. G. F. Brandon, London, 1970; art. *Intercession*, by J. Robson, p. 360.
11 *Dalā'il*, p. 42, 44 and 48.
12 See further the present writer's, *Islām: A Christian Perspective*, p. 13, on 'Barnabas'. As far as the ancient 'apocryphal' Gospels are concerned, the one definite reference in the *Qur'ān* is to the 'Infancy Gospel of Thomas', (Q 3:49). The *Qurān* seems to depend upon this Gospel for its account of the infant Jesus making birds of clay and then breathing life into them. The Christology of this Gospel can hardly be said to be reductionist!
13 In fairness, however, we must remember that many Muslims would regard *Muḥammad* as an ideal *precisely* because of his worldly concerns. For them, Jesus is too far removed from the concerns of ordinary men and women to be a model.
14 See further Chapter 2, 'Christology in an Islāmic Context'.

PART IV: Chapter 15

1 A. J. Malik, 'Church-State Relationships', Paper read to the Communicators Fellowship, 9th April, 1983.
2 H. Chadwick, *The Early Church*, p. 47.
3 Ibid., p. 50.
4 See further W. H. C. Frend, *The Early Church*, London, 1965, p. 50f.
5 W. G. Young, *Patriarch, Shah and Caliph*, p. 30f., 154.
6 Iris H. El Masry, *The Coptic Church*, Cairo, 1977, p. 63.
7 Young, *op. cit.*, p. 36.
8 J. Maritain, *Christianity and Democracy*, London, 1946, p. 29–30.
9 See further E. Brunner, *Christianity and Civilization*, Vol. 11, London, 1955, p. 120.
10 See Eric Massey's paper, 'Islāmic Constitution', pp. 2, 3, IV.
11 The Ordinance of *'Umar* is a code that restricts quite severely the rights of non-Muslim minorities. See further the present writer's *Islām: A Christian Perspective*, p. 38.
12 E. Massey, ibid., pp. 2–3: 2c, d.
13 *Qur'ān* 2:30, 33:72.
14 'Islāmic Constitution', pp. 1:3.

PART IV: Chapter 16

1 M. Black (ed.), *Peake's Commentary on the Bible,* art. *Exodus,* D. M. G. Stalker, London, 1962, p. 230.
2 On the relationship between the Mosaic Law and other ancient legal codes, see R. K. Harrison, *Old Testament Times,* London, 1971, p. 153ff.
3 R. De Vaux, *Ancient Israel: Its Life and Institutions,* London, 1961, p. 140f.
4 W. Barclay, *Matthew,* Vol. 1, Edinburgh, 1975, p. 146f.
5 N. J. Coulson, *A History of Islāmic Law,* Edinburgh, 1864, p. 18.
6 Lahore, 1963, pp XXIV.
7 *Abū A'lā Maudūdī, Rights of Non-Muslims in an Islāmic State,* Lahore, 1978, p. 12; see also *Dā'ira Ma'ārif-Islāmia,* Vol. 16:2, Lahore, 1978, p. 173f.; also *Encyclopaedia of Islām,* Vol. II, London, 1965, art. 'Diya', p. 70f.
8 Bligh, *The Sermon on the Mount,* Slough, 1975, p. 70f.
9 D. Kidner, *Hard Sayings: The Challenge of Old Testament Morals,* London, 1972, p. 14.
10 Luke 19:1–10.
11 op. cit., pp. 37–38.
12 'The Humanitarian Theory of Punishment,' reprint from 'Res Judicate' in *Churchmen Speak,* Marcham Manor Press, 1966, p. 39f.
13 Kidner, op. cit., p. 39.

PART IV: Chapter 17

1 Gen. 1:26–30; 2:24–28.
2 Q 2:30, 33:72.
3 Gen. 15:6, Rom. 4:3, Gal. 3:6; cf. Rom. 6:15–19, Gal. 5:13–15, Jas. 2:28f.
4 See the present writer's *Islām: A Christian Perspective,* p. 95f. and 124f.
5 I owe the term to the Rev. Robert Wilkes. See further an old but important work on the subject: J. C. Heinrich, *The Psychology of a Suppressed People,* London, 1937.
6 J. C. England, *Living Theology in Asia,* SCM, London, 1981; V. Samuel and C. Sugden (eds.), *Sharing Jesus in the Two Thirds World;* K. Y. Bock (ed.), *Minjung Theology,* Singapore, CCA, 1981.
7 Rom. Ch. 8, Phil. 2:12–13. See further, the Anglican-Roman Catholic International Commissions report '*Salvation and the Church*', London, 1987.
8 Matt. 5:38f.
9 e.g. Amos, Matt. 23, 25.
10 See for example, Leon Howell, *People are the Subject,* CWME-WCC, Geneva, 1980.
11 See further *Your Kingdom Come,* CWME-WCC, Geneva, 1980.
12 K. Kitamori, *Theology of the Pain of God,* Richmond, Virginia, U.S.A., p. 965.
13 Matt. 5:11, 10:16f., 20:23, John 21:18f; cf. 2 Cor. 4:7–12.

Index of Authors

Study Guide to Doctrines, Qualities & Titles

General Subject Index

Index of Biblical References

OLD TESTAMENT

NEW TESTAMENT

Index of References To The Qur'ān